PLEASURES OF LOVING

Plaisirs D'Amour – Almanach erotique des femmes was first published in Paris in 1982. It presents a vivid picture of the sex dreams and experiences of contemporary French women, as supplied by the readers of the internationally respected magazine *Elle*. From the crude and the kinky, to the poetic and the perverse, this collection is both challenging and titillating – and the unmistakable product of the female imagination.

PLEASURES OF LOVING

Compiled by Maren Sell

Translated by Nicholas Courtin

A STAR BOOK
published by
the Paperback Division of
W. H. ALLEN & Co. PLC

A Star Book
Published in 1986
by the Paperback Division of
W. H. Allen & Co. PLC
44 Hill Street, London W1X 8LB

Copyright © Lieu Commun 1982
Translation copyright © W. H. Allen 1986
Printed and bound in Great Britain by
Anchor Brendon Ltd, Tiptree, Essex

ISBN 0 352 31680 2

LOVE PLAY

Stream Of Love

The day was a sultry yellow. And so was I. We lay in that meadow among the wild flowers listening to the stream bubbling a hundred yards away, and I couldn't take my eyes off you. I was mesmerized by your lovely chestnut eyes with their dark buttons. You were staring at me too, your pupils dilated and boring into me. We were naked and looking forward to making love.

You seemed drowsy, lethargic. But the moment came when I wanted you physically, longed to touch your skin and of course your stiff thing jutting out from the red-brown hairs between your thighs. I kept glancing at that swollen powerful thing and suddenly now I wanted it. Carefully I brought my head down to your knees, and a for a while I breathed in the tang of the sun on your legs. I slid up to your penis, and eased your bag free, with its sweaty man smell. I took one of the little balls between my lips, and you were afraid for an instant, knowing that I could bite it and hurt you. Such a vulnerable part! I let it go and nudged it again two, three, four times to see the skin of your scrotum tighten. Then took the other one.

You were reassured, and I could feel you enjoying it, because of your tiny twitches of pleasure. Then without warning I put my tongue out and slithered it along the gossamer smooth stem that was slightly curved, the skin taut. I wanted to make your prick grow bigger, but all it did was quiver. I licked it for ages thinking I must look like a cow, glad you couldn't see. I was trembling too now and I found it hard to breathe. I carefully pulled back the funny little skin on the end and ran the tip of my tongue round the secret crease where the gland begins, then under the skin. I heard you holding your breath and I withdrew, stopping a moment to admire the blueish veins along the stem, pumping like those on your wrist. I kissed the gland itself, now reddish and exposed. With my tongue's tip I worried the miniscule hole where your sperm would spurt, opaque and fecund. We were both shaking and I opened my mouth really wide to let your pipe slip in, strong and round and thick and raw. The smell and taste of it as I swallowed it and withdrew again, and again, almost made me come. But I was patient, and let it flop out for a while. Then I descended to the base and nipped it with my lips, then teased it at the top again and finally took it right to the back of my throat. You started whimpering and gabbling incoherently, asking me to go on. Obediently I sucked with all my strength, until I could actually feel your veins pumping and I knew you were coming. Seconds later your stuff spurted inside my mouth, tasting bitter somehow, and your middle heaved up and down and you threw your head back and gasped. I didn't want to swallow your fluid, but it was hard not to with your thing going on pumping. I waited until it died down and then withdrew and let the fluid spill out. To my surprise the shaft jerked some more and some white liquid came out. My adoring eyes enveloped you, I loved your pleasure so!

You took my hand and we lay side by side. It was wonderful lying in the flowers. The grass had that gorgeous hay smell, and we listened to the gurgling stream and watched a bee being seduced by a bell flower. Time stood still. Then our eyes met, you gave my hand a squeeze and hoisted yourself onto your side, caressing my face and pausing on my lips while I kissed the finger. You kept brushing my lips and I felt weak and kissed the finger repeatedly.

You leaned over, my love, and placed your mouth on mine, forcing your tongue inside. I parted my lips and you went deeper. It was heaven when you gave me some saliva and I swallowed it. My hands were all over you and I had to clench my legs, I was so excited. I couldn't wait for that other penetration I knew would be soon, but you kept licking and running your tongue over mine. I could feel your hand stroking my legs, touching my waist and under my arms. At last you reached my breasts and took them with your firm hands, and I knew the tips were engorged and hard. I wish you'd nip them I said, but you just kept

8

on. Funny feelings started lower down and that's where you shifted your attentions, to my abdomen, so that I caught my breath.

I could wait no longer, but you went slowly, cruelly, and made me respond to your slightest gesture, I was ahead of you but your finger tips merely fluttered around my little flower. I was aware of the lips there swelling and I was sure I was moist, but I experienced an instant of anguish wondering if the flower would open for you. Your finger nudged my tiny button and I knew I was wet with dew. In masterful fashion you gripped my shoulders and covered me with your whole body, your arms and legs heavy on mine, forcing my thighs apart. You raised yourself a little and I glimpsed your huge sinewy thing waiting to plunge into me. You touched the fleece with your thing and gave a couple of pushes to make me open up. A third push and your enormous male part came right into me! Oh bliss, I could feel it rubbing inside and it didn't hurt at all. Your middle moved back and forth. I was living each centimetre of each stroke, but you stopped, perhaps scared of coming too soon, but I said please go on! I could feel myself near the brink, I clenched you with my thighs but it was too difficult. All I knew was that you were filling my whole lower torso, you were possessing me, wanting me, wanting me, wanting me! Desecrating my hallowed spot!!

We were drenched in perspiration, and I loved that. Loved it too when you had to stop and I writhed underneath you, making your hot thing squirm about in my vagina. Desire came in waves and I seemed to be pulsing from my anus to my sex and on as far as my neck. Completely mellow, I could hardly say what I felt. Your thigh and chest muscles tightened and you plunged into me in a final assault. Ah yes, I felt that, how big you must be! My sex was a yard wide and my legs splayed on the grass, when you shouted, 'Ah' and your big pump gushed within me. I caught sight of your eyes glinting as you spent yourself, then I went into a sort of coma.

The first of the crickets began their song soon afterwards, and I wanted to stay there for hours listening to them and the stream. Sadly it became quite chilly, and we realized we had to get back, not telling anyone where we had been.

Nelly

My Golden Boy

I felt itchy all that morning, bitchy somehow. Then I thought of the waggon.

A few weeks before I had been walking through the woods with my husband, and we came across an old waggon in among the undergrowth, with a chimney thing sticking out, and someone had made a kind of window on one side. It was an enchanting hovel of a place, and I wanted to push the door open, it was swaying a little in the wind, I wanted to go inside. But my husband said it would not be right, it was none of our business.

And now, on that particular day, he was away on business! I was free until the weekend and had this yen to spend the night in the waggon. Too bad if he phoned, I'd think of something. Happy as a little girl out from school, I strode along the track leading to the waggon, inhaling the fragrance of the leaves and the earth and the mushrooms. When I reached the place, nothing had altered, so I pushed the door open gingerly. Once accustomed to the dark interior I found I was not the first: a rucksack, a sleeping bag and a layer of dry ferns were on the ground. I threw off my travel bag and lay down on the ferns, breathing in their pungent smell. It was hot outside and the sun was unnaturally bright, too bright, flaring enough to herald a storm. The forest seemed to be waiting for it, sensing its proximity. I was enjoying my escapade, and would wait for the other person.

Whoever it was, they were taking their time. At least half an hour must have gone by and the initial contentment, the desire to hug myself in excitement, was fading. I sighed and breathed in deeply, noticing as I did so that my bosom was rather more prominent than usual, which of course is something that happens at a certain stage in the month. It really was a shapely bosom and I took off my T-shirt to admire it. Then found I was undoing the buttons on the top of my shorts. It was so hot. Then I flushed, knowing what I really wanted. There was no reason not to, and I suppose I was influenced by the fact that I was wearing a G-string and felt sexy. My hand slid inside the shorts down to the triangle of material at the front, then underneath that. I touched my silky little thatch down there, finding it moist already. My fingers began playing, idly stroking the lips, insinuating themselves into the warm submissive crack. I rubbed faster, all along the aperture and located my button and dwelt there. It had all happened so swiftly, but I liked the idea of doing it here deep in the woods. In due course the familiar tingle of desire came and I circled and stroked, meaning to make the pleasure last. If anyone came I would hear them, and could feign sleep.

It was when I was concentrating most and breathing harder that I sensed I was not alone. Maybe it was just the door creaking in the breeze. Anyhow I ignored it and closed my eyes, certain I could come easily this time. I gave free rein to my fantasies, and just at the crucial moment another hand slipped into my shorts and took over from mine! A man's hand! I came instantly, powerless to control the climax, rasping and gulping in air in quick sequence, so violent was the orgasm. Longing for it to go on, I arched my back and forced my quim against the unknown hand. The fingers were gentle but firm, vibrating expertly on my nicest spot. Regaining my composure, I felt the man's breath on my cheek and turned in the fading light to see the imprecise features, not of a man, but of a male god bronzed from the sun.

He was really very young, definitely my junior, with blond curly hair and honest eyes that I found quite irresistible, although I was not sure of the colour in the dark. This magnificent boy fumbled and tugged to remove my shorts, and I squirmed to help him. He was going to take me for himself this time! I sat there naked except for my socks and shoes, and he lifted a breast, pinching the nipple erect and then kissing it, rubbing it with his lips until it hurt a bit, and then sucking it greedily like a baby claiming its rights. I, the 'mother', glowed with pleasure throughout my body. My legs seemed sore, my toes curled under, my womb grew tight and I gave a series of bites to my baby's neck.

Shifting his position, he lowered me and gave me a languid kiss, immediately forced open my knees and probed against my thatch with his hard imperious organ. The youth's cock demanded access, and he penetrated me a little and moved back and forth. After a few thrusts, I found myself bucking up at him, trying to make him go deeper. But he held back, expertly moving his gland from side to side, then a little farther into my tunnel. I wanted to make it last but I wanted him to go deeper as well – I was unsure exactly what I did want! And suddenly he was moving like a piston and I was meeting him, imagining him growing enormous, and then actually feeling him swell. It was I who came first, I think, I really cannot say because I simply shut my eyes and saw sheet lightning as he grunted and spent himself within me. I pictured the sperm shooting out viscously, profusely, and then the white light turned to grey-green and I was unable to move. I remember he squeezed my hand and I drifted off, floating high up into nothingness.

It was night when I awoke. He had a gas lamp going and a horse-blanket was keeping me warm. The youth looked at me with his bright eyes. I felt like a kid with a new toy – a boy with finely muscled shoulders and arms. I blinked and looked back at him.

Only then did he speak, and I could understand nothing. It sounded German. His voice was brown with happiness and that was enough for me. His joy erupted into a laugh and I laughed too. I was radiant.

I felt thirsty and he handed me a can of beer. As I sipped it he caressed my hair, and I ran a couple of fingers down his cheek and over a shoulder, wanting to be kissed again. We examined each other, but he did not move. How I longed to make love again! I sipped some more beer and put the can down. I placed my lips against his cheek. He responded with a chaste peck and I feared it might all be over. However, he slid under the blanket with me, his unclothed torso and thighs giving off heat, but so soft to the touch. He began handling my bottom and I felt his prick hard against my abdomen. Tender as a child and yet with male authority, he forced my thighs open, and I was

13

telling him yes by tugging at his curls. I was looking forward to him taking longer this second time. His open mouth brushed my neck and shoulders and sucked at both breasts in turn. It was heavenly and as he moved, his rod, much redder this time, kept touching my belly. Hungrily I found it, squeezed its bigness and felt the beat of it, then guided it to my entrance. It was up to him now, and he hesitated, and I said, 'Please, please,' aching for him to slide it in like he did before, wanting him to want me and have his pleasure from me. Then he pushed my knees back and I stopped breathing as he came into me with a single thrust, deeper than before. Again he held back, so that waves of hot delight surged through me, before he finally lost control and possessed me for the second time, muttering harshly.

We listened to the wind in the trees. He sighed once or twice and we laughed. Then we got out our food and drank beer from the same glass, sitting like a pair of tailors, our genitalia rudely exposed. We made the moment last, but eventually put our clothes on. He told me his name, Hans, and I told him my name was Sophie. We could say nothing further which was good because, after love-making, it's usually something banal and fairly pointless. He led me outside, and at first I could see absolutely nothing, just hear the wind and the noise of some animal scurrying away. The trees began to take shape as we strolled along, his arm on my shoulders, mine round his waist, and me feeling small beside him. We stopped at a clearing and there was a large pond with a wan moon mirrored in it. A few stray leaves floated on the water and there were some tree trunks and some rushes. It was dreamy, the sky was humid and an owl hooted a few times.

Hans was in no hurry to move, letting me enjoy the atmosphere; I had given him pleasure, he gave me the pond, the night, the forest and the owl. I like owls and wished I could make friends with this one. Wished, too, that I could tell Hans what fun it was, instead of which I squeezed his hand and laid my head against his arms. I whispered, 'Hans' and he whispered, 'Sophie' with a catch in his voice, and we thought how wonderful it was being there. His finger explored my face and he gave me another kiss that went on and on so that I forgot the night, the trees and the water.

A jagged flash made the trees stand out starkly, and the heavens grumbled. We were sitting on a tree stump, my companion holding me tight with his cheek in my hair. The wind was getting up and the storm seemed noisier. Then the first drops of rain fell and we ran helter-skelter for the waggon, where Hans lit the lamp again, putting it behind his rucksack so that it wouldn't dazzle us. He arranged his sleeping bag as a large bed, and we giggled because we were cosy. Because we were playing a lovely game.

Then – a miracle – he was wooing me again, eager once more to exchange the glorious sting of pleasure. How could he be so ardent, I wondered, and felt as timid as a little girl about to be kissed for the first time. I was sitting with my knees up on the edge of the sleeping bag, and Hans drew near, fondled my hair and lifted my chin. I believe I actually gaped as his gaze held me. My lover planted tiny kisses all over my face and a finger traced a line down my neck, my shoulder, my arm and across to the nearest breast. I was trembling and my quim was contracting in anticipation in little jumps. He stood me up and undressed me gently, carefully and lovingly and I adored being adored. Meanwhile I could admire his handsome features at an angle, his cheekbones and strong chin. A shadow cast itself prettily across my breasts, and I stood naked before him, and he fully dressed. But I kept still, fearing to spoil it, for men can become timid for unaccountable reasons. So I watched him take his things off, down to his tight-fitting pants with his penis jutting out erotically. And desiring me! He paused, and I took down his final garment, easing out his shaft, worrying it so that it swelled and the veins traced wiggly paths along it. We rolled onto the sleeping bag and I ran my lips down his penis. This time by tacit agreement it was I who would have him. I forced my lips right down his thing, dribbling and making it wet and gulping at it so that the bulging pulpy end filled my throat. His fierce male smell joined the earth's fragrance, driving me wild with lust for him. I had to come up for air, and he shifted to lick my own crease as I crouched on all fours panting. I was the female on heat and he was my stallion, my bull, my male pig. I in turn shifted and squatted down on his cock, impaling my haunches on it, joggling up and down on it, making it rub my clitoris. Crying real tears I grabbed at his shoulders, digging my nails into the flesh, bumping up and down on him trying to flatten my pubis onto his bone. My entire body was afire as I went on heaving and he arched in rhythm. Each descent was more thrilling than the one before, each withdrawal more tantalising. Behind my squeals I vaguely heard thunder and there were some flashes outside, but I had only one object in mind – getting an orgasm from my male sex object. I felt it coming and coming like a huge soreness that overwhelmed me. I lost count, perhaps it was just one long explosion-implosion – I don't know what!

We lay still for ages after that, the rain drumming on the roof, the wind whipping through the trees and throwing the branches at one other with a crack. One peal of thunder was louder than all the others, and I clutched at Hans, so that our still-wet organs touched. The tempest blew itself out and gave way to steady drizzle. I went to sleep with my head nestling in his armpit while he whispered in German.

I came to in broad daylight, alone under the blanket. More precisely, the sun stayed outside but I could see the bright clean sky through the window and the raindrops on the leaves and branches. The birds were chirruping their heads off. The aroma of coffee reached me and I was reassured, my golden boy was still there and would become a boy scout and hand me a drink within seconds; which he did with a smile that made my heart leap. 'Bonshour,' he said in his charming accent and we drank deep, afterwards throwing the mugs to the side, and ourselves at each other under the blanket for a last cuddle. The last? It was not to be. Stimulated by the freshness of the morning, we threw off the blanket and were kneeling face to face, touching each other and impatient to do it again.

With no word spoken, I found I had turned my back to him, intuitively knowing what he wanted to do. A hand glided round to play with my boobies, now seemingly bigger than ever, while the other rubbed me firmly and rhythmically between my legs. I felt his dry open mouth on my neck and then in the small of my back. He pushed me forward and parted my buttocks, running his tongue repeatedly up my crack and worrying the entrance there. I had never been sodomised before and was terrified when his stiff rod slide across my bottom. A finger squirmed at the entrance to my back passage and then went inside, exploring. I pleaded with him not to hurt me and he said *'Nein!'* and I knew I could trust him. With an effort of will I loosened up, and suddenly the tip of his penis was just inside. Instinctively I jerked forward, it seemed so enormous, but his hand on my pubis prevented me rejecting him. This same hand was rubbing me fiercely and I gave myself up to him. He would have his way come what may, I knew, and I had no choice but to surrender. I shall never forget that penetration, during which I felt every contour of his member inching itself deeper, almost painfully but not really. How much bigger would it get?!

In an effort to relax I kept telling myself this was dirty, naughty, sinful and that had its effect, for I even began pushing back against him, then harder and harder until he was huge and actually hurting. But the ache was so delicious I did not protest, but melted completely, I shouted incoherently when I came, his penis now thrusting and his fingers inside my vagina. I felt him spurt and rasp, out of control. I tried to clench him at the base with the ring of my anus, and he stayed firm for ages, so that I seemed to have a continuous orgasm. I was so happy!

I dozed on the ferns, enjoying my soreness, and Hans cooked some potatoes in their jackets in some embers. These we ate in silence, on the edge of the pond, occasionally glancing at each other. His eyes were hazel, I discovered.

17

Back in the hut I got my travel bag and Hans knew I had made up my mind to leave now. He made no attempt to stop me, not even saying '*Au revoir*'. He kissed me a long moment with infinite tenderness, and we walked a few yards. I hugged him to me and left at once. I looked back, of course, just once. We would never see each other again, but I was replete with joy, already thinking of other adventures to come. Adventures like this one with no problems, no strings attached, no tomorrows.

Sophie

Office Fun

Directly I set eyes on him I knew we would become much more than two people in the same firm. A girl can sense those things at once, and I said: 'I'll make him sooner or later, I will. It's just a matter of patience and waiting as long as you have to.'

It's always the same technique really. You lay the foundations and just carry through the plan step by step. It never fails. Although I had my doubts this time because his job obliged him to leave early in the morning before we secretaries arrived, and get back late in the evening. I would have to do the best I could in the circumstances.

I started the job in mid-year, and allowed myself a little time to settle in. It was best to sniff around a bit and, as it was the holidays in August for the others, I simply watched him and made a few first approaches, like smiling and walking past him and such. It's very important to study people when you want to get somewhere with them. You have to flatter them by revealing details about themselves.

The holidays went by and I prepared to attack, because I wasn't too sure about staying with that firm more than a year and I didn't want to leave without, well, something to remember it by.

He was the one who started it when he addressed me one day with the familiar 'tu'. I seized the chance and from that moment I said 'tu' too. Some of the others were a bit toffee-nosed about it, the very idea of a 21-year-old kid just come through the front door using 'tu' to a chap of 34 with a pretty senior position! So I began being far more relaxed with him, and the prospects looked good. As the days went by we unwound and started chatting as if we had known each other for ages.

Then January 19th arrived. I was not feeling at all well and I sort of groped my way through the day. Things seemed to pitch around and I thought I would pass out. It started when I went down to his office, where I almost fainted and he rushed up to make sure I didn't slip over. It was all quite natural, and I found myself in his kind sweet arms. He wanted to take me home to my place. Later he admitted he thought I was drunk. Quite the lady I must have seemed!

But that was only messing around, and I really discovered he had taken a fancy to me one day in his office when he was on the phone and I got close to him and he put his arm round my waist.

The next few days were very similar. Each time I went to see him and we were alone he used to do nice little things to me. Nothing that could harm either of us, nothing to worry about. And then on February 4th I said to myself: 'Maybe we're going to get something practical out of this!'

It's funny how in some ways he was still a boy in spite of his age. The day he took my hand and squeezed it hard in his, I asked myself whether he was 34 or 14.

February 10th was a bad day, when he was not on form. No little kisses or tenderness or anything. Something must have been wrong! But the next day he made up for it. When I got to his office he pushed me against the wall, gently, just to say hello. And soon after that, when I went down to show him a file, he got up and went behind me and folded his arms around me.

Well, it was not always easy and we were very careful nobody caught us. It was obvious that people would not understand. I didn't care, had nothing to lose and more likely something to gain. But very quickly I let myself be trapped, and realized it was him making the advances. After that things became more serious, and he got to caressing me, casually, feeling my tit as he went by, then while he was phoning, and it became an everyday thing and I paid no further attention to it. Our conversation became more carefree and daring, but still proper. He knew he couldn't rush me.

On February 16th we talked about the hottest part of the human body, in a philosophical kind of way. I suggested the lower back and the sides of the abdomen, saying I had experience of it. His dinger was bursting through his body suit!

On February 18th he asked me: 'When are you going to

wear a skirt?' He stroked my thighs through my trousers, his fingers gradually travelling up. Above that I wore a blouse, but when his fingers wriggled through past the buttons he found a little waistcoat thing underneath. The phone rang and that was that. So he just left his hand on my side without moving it. The steady type!

On February 23rd I came in with my dress with the thigh slits and we discussed for and against, and I said I thought about it from experience.

'I like your dress a lot,' he said, slipping his hand in the slit. I came over all candy-floss.

We giggled for a bit and a colleague came in. Stupidly we were caught out and we made a mess of covering it up. The other person, a woman, left quickly.

'You'd think she listened at keyholes,' he said.

'Maybe she'll leave us in peace now,' I replied.

On February 26th when I arrived he was cutting his nails, as he was careful not to ladder my tights. But it didn't stop him creeping up high under my skirt, and we had a long giggle about it. At times we were like two kids, and I thought it was super.

Then it was March 2nd, the afternoon I broke my brooch, and when I went down and saw he was back, he noticed it right away. A good sign!

He said: 'Who's done that, someone been playing about with you?'

'Huh,' I said sharp as you like, 'who's been touching the boss's dolly bird?' It was only said in fun but his mouth twisted into a zig-zag.

'I'm a jealous chap, you know, don't like others straying onto my territory, front or back.'

You could have knocked me down. I sort of glowed, being his property like, at any rate so he thought. I had to chuckle though; it's always the married ones who are the most possessive, especially when they're deceiving their wives. Awful, they are.

Next day when he was on the phone again, he slid his arm round my bottom and then held my hand, our fingers entwined romantically.

He suddenly jumped: 'I've no hand left to write.'

21

'Oh don't let me interfere with your work,' said I, and we giggled.

The day after that he gave me a new brooch, and told me no-one else was to lay his hands on it. Well naturally there was nothing I could say to that, and to cut a long story short he invited me for a drive out in his car and I said I would come if he got some of the mud off it.

That brought us to March 5th and he obviously took it seriously, telling me he'd had the car cleaned up. 'Why, something special?' I said, innocent. He said: 'You told me you didn't want to make love in a dirty car.' And I said: 'Not in any car, if you please.' Which was ambiguous, and he called me a 'bourgeoise', and I let him have a little squeeze. I jut out at several points but only two of them are breasts.

Bourgeoise or no bourgeoise, with all the pawing around I started to smell his body odour on my clothes in the morning. He smelt pretty strong, like some men do, and I was scared it would give us away.

A few days after that he worked the chat round to the shape of people's bottoms, saying he didn't like them flat and that my cheeks were real Brigitte Bardot class. When she was my age of course.

'When am I going to see them?' he asked outright. And I said: 'You in a hurry or something?' and he said: 'Oo, hoity-toity!'

Then he got serious and I had to make up my mind. I was leaving his office and he stepped in front of the door. This could be it! I went up and put my hands on his shirt front, letting one creep up to a shoulder, getting a feel of his left tit on the way, just for the interest. I took a step forward so I was pressed against him, and laid my chin on his shoulder. He let his head go back, and our cheeks were together. He played round the back of my neck and we stayed like that a bit. I kept my distance after that until March 15th when I woke up quite randy and went in early, finding him in his office reading a paper. I went up behind him and ran my arms round his middle, with my cheek against his. Closing the gender gap!

'Goodmorning, handsome, how're you feeling?' I said,

giving him a wet kiss on the neck.

Then on March 17th I remarked that there was no light any more hanging from the ceiling. 'That shows you don't look when you come in here,' he said, and I quipped back: 'Shows I have eyes only for you, love.'

Anyway, on March 22nd, he tried his luck upstairs in the room I worked in, coming up to my chair and slipping his hand into my V-neck shirt and then right under my bra. He fondled my bosom and I had to tell him: 'Remember we're liable to have company.' He took his hand away then.

He wasn't too sure how far I'd let him go, but on April 21st he tried the door technique again in his office, and I stumbled against him accidentally on purpose so that we were cheek-to-cheek and he was kissing my neck and I was running my hands over his shirt. I kissed his neck too and made out there was nothing special to it.

Finally on April 22nd he went a bit red and said: 'About time we made love.'

'When you like.' I'd had enough of canoodling.

'Good, right away!'

I got angry and said: 'What are you playing at? Can't you be serious? You start something and spoil it.'

He drew me to him and said he was sorry. But he kept on making little suggestions, and on April 23rd I told him: 'Listen, if you can't go through with it, stop saying things, dangling me on a string.'

That evening he said, 'About your date, think of me, and I'll be thinking of you when I'm doing it.' Meaning with his wife. Then he held me very tight and growled: 'Whenever I do it with her, I'm really making love with you now.'

'It's the same with me, but we mustn't worry about it.'

On May 14th he told me: 'I'm off all next week on holiday, what are you going to do, will you be lonely?' It was a lousy week, I didn't feel like doing anything and hardly ate anything.

It was hot on June 11th and he was very worked up: 'My God, I'd like to . . .' then on June 15th he must have been thinking about it all day because he burst in saying: 'I'll

23

teach you to go on teasing like you do, I'm going to rape you over the chair.' But nothing came of it.

On June 24th we were interrupted twice during the morning while we were starting to neck. But when everyone had gone, I said: 'Where did we get to?' He smiled at that, and I leaned over him and slid my hand down, undoing his shirt buttons and caressing his belly, reaching right down to his bush.

'I didn't do it on purpose,' I said, 'and you know you like it.'

I had other things on my mind during July and we did practically nothing. I tried my best to be nice to him, but it was obvious I wanted it more than he did.

But I wasn't giving up. It was my turn to go on holiday, and it was going to be tough not seeing him for a month. I only hoped he would not find some other playmate while I was away. I can be jealous too, a real tigress!

Actually, I was still almost a virgin, you might say.

It was great being on holiday. The sun shone day after day and I was determined to enjoy myself. Among all these strangers it ought not to be too difficult finding someone. Mind you, I was going to have to work at it. To tell the truth I was wondering whether I was not spontaneous enough, as you might say, because when you're lying on the beach getting a tan, you don't really feel like making an effort and put it off to the next day. All the same I genuinely wanted to make love, I felt sort of creamy in the solar plexus.

I was strolling along trying to work something out when a car nearly ran over me. It was my fault, I didn't look as I went across, being wrapped up in myself. Then I heard the screech of the tyres and I looked back to see what I'd done. And to my surprise, it was him. He wound the window down and I went back.

'What a coincidence! What are you doing here of all places?'

'I'm on holiday, remember? What about you?'

Cars were building up behind and blowing their horns.

'Get in,' he said, and thrust the door open.

24

'Where are we going?'

'Out of everybody's way for a start, and then to some quieter spot.'

We drove for a few minutes and there was no sign of the quiet spot. 'Where are you taking me?' I said, starting to get quite worried.

'It's a surprise, you'll see.'

'You're not taking me to Bordeaux, I hope.'

'Sure I'm not, in fact here we are.' He switched off and we got out. It was in an area just made up of private houses, and it seemed very quiet, although the sea was only a short distance away at the end of the garden. Then I remembered he mentioned he had a villa round this way.

'I had to come down and pick up a few things. Won't keep you long,' he said, much brighter now that he was away from the office.

'Take your time, I've nothing special to rush about for,' I said, also cheerful.

'In any case, we can have a drink while you're here. I think there's some inside, but it won't be chilled.' We were inside by now. 'Just open the shutters if you can, so we can see the place.'

I went to the first window: 'I'm not sure how this works ...'

Suddenly there was a scraping noise of a chair, and I looked round and he took me in his arms, rubbing his neck against mine.

'It's a long time since we saw each other, how are you?' he said, giving me a kiss or two on my neck. 'Are you missing me, or have you found someone else to keep you happy?'

He took my hand and tugged it, leading me further into the house. It was completely dark, and he didn't say any more, and nor did I. Eventually I began to distinguish things, but just then he opened a door and drew me into a room, and I realized it was a bedroom, with a low bed. He flung himself onto his back and pulled me down with him. I made no resistance and he started fingering my sari at the top, on one shoulder. He said it was a pretty dress and I told him it was a sari from India. Fat fingers strayed

25

around and the material was so thin I could feel their heat, especially as I was feeling a little chilly in the closed-up room. At the office it had taken him so long, and now he was trying to make me like some playboy, fondling me all down my back and round my bottom and then stroking my breasts. I was so surprised that I let out a squeak and he thought I was laughing at him

'What's so funny? Am I really that comical?'

'I'm not laughing,' I breathed, getting up on one arm and giving him a tender kiss on his forehead. That was enough for him!

He drew me to him and we rolled over so that his big thigh went between my legs, and he took my breath away as he kissed me lots of times on my shoulders and over my face, finally putting his lips against mine and forcing them open. His tongue slithered in and I let him explore me with the tip. He was really very forceful and without me realizing it he unknotted my sari, pulling it down, then turning me over and removing my sari completely. As a matter of fact I moved to make it easier for him, and eventually he had me lying face down and there was no doubt he was going to skip his siesta today!

'You have a lovely soft skin,' he declared, massaging my back and tapping my bottom so that I could feel it wobbling like a jelly.

'I had it when I was a baby,' I said.

I felt weak, and must have looked pale, but of course it didn't show. My whole chest was tight, as I realized what I was doing, a young girl with this man 13 years older than her, who was making her on his bed. I started quivering a bit, and knew I was getting worked up.

I was beginning to like these preliminaries and I said: 'Know any more tricks like that?'

He stopped squeezing my behind for a second: 'Plenty more I could teach you if you'd like to try learning.'

'Oh yes, I am a studious girl and I'm sure I would learn fast.'

I had to admit that I had plenty to learn where petting was concerned, and I was only too willing for him to act as my tutor. For a year we had been touching each other up and there was a kind of complicity between us, so that as we lay on the bed there was no need to talk. We knew by telepathy what to do and in no time at all he drew me on top of him, and looked at my breasts hanging down like small melons with the nipples sticking out. My legs were on his and he forced his knees up so that my own parted, and I could feel his thing poking up against the crack in my bottom.

'Let's get in the bed,' he said, sort of grumbling.

'What for, this is lovely like this. You're not cold are you?'

'No but I always have to have something over me.'

'If that's your problem, won't I do instead of the sheet?'

Immediately he got me onto my back, and my arms were clutching him. I was nervous but forced myself to take it easy. Perhaps if we talked some more I would relax, I thought.

'Your skin's lovely too,' I said, raising my head slightly to be kissed. He crushed my lips and then moved to my breasts. Magic messages flowed all over my body, as he kissed me everywhere, returning to suck my left breast, doing it hard and taking in a whole mouthful of flesh.

'Oh be careful, that's very tender and I want to keep it,' I exclaimed.

'I wouldn't hurt you,' he murmured, licking the nipple to make it better.

'But you are,' I shouted, and this was the cue for us to pretend we were fighting. We pinched and pulled each other, laughing and panting. He smacked me on my bottom and I cried out, and then he was was kneeling over me and forcing his ramrod into me. I lay back motionless as he pushed it in and out, but not hurting at all, even slowing down and I really liked that. I never imagined he could do it so well, and in a way it was the first time ever for me, at least properly. I would advise any girl to make sure the chap is experienced the first time, it's so much more – enriching! Neither of us said, 'I love you' or anything like that, and there was no need to. I came first, and then he sort of ransacked me. I felt marvellous afterwards.

He got off my body and lay face down next to me, but his

hand was in mine, both of them wet with sweat. I decided to get up soon and sat on the bed, moving his hand away.

'What's the matter?' he mumbled, rising to a kneeling position and kissing me on the neck.

I could only stammer, I was a bit lost: 'I-er-I want ...'

'You what?' he said.

'To do it again,' I said. Silly really, but I'm not too poetic.

We did it again, and I was amazed that I liked it so much. With boys I had always done it to please them, even if I didn't get off myself. I felt like a badly brought up little girl doing something naughty.

After a while I said I wanted to do it a third time, and he said he couldn't and I said of course he could. I was glad, because it was different every time.

I had no idea of the time, but he said: 'Well I'll have to get back now.'

'Already? Oh no,' I pleaded.

Of course it was scheming, but I wanted to show him I was prepared to make love with him again some other time. So I played the tart and kissed him a lot, telling him with my mouth he could have me whenever he wanted.

For a long while we lay there with our eyes shut.

'I must fly now, it's late,' he said, giving me a peck and starting to get dressed.

We put the bed straight and shut the place up, so there was no evidence.

For days I wondered whether we had actually done what we did, whether we had simply had a drink together in the kitchen.

Violette Puech

On all Fours

I knew a tall young man with a body full of sap, and I badly wanted him. It was one of those weeks. I sent him a letter inviting him for the evening, written in my schoolgirl handwriting and explaining exactly what I wanted him to do.

I was worried whether he would come at all, and whether he would understand what I was getting at. I spent the whole day wandering about the house waiting for the evening, agitated and feeling so sexy I was actually clammy.

It was difficult to know what to wear. Would a fancy man's shirt of the thinnest cotton turn him on, or a see-through sheath dress, or tight jeans? In the end I slipped into a light dress in a smooth material, and wore nothing underneath? Why not? I sometimes went out like that.

I was waiting for the bell to ring, and opened the door to find him smiling nicely, kindly, looking at me with a sort of dancing yellow sparkle in his green eyes. I knew he was up to it, I can smell vigour in a man. He was holding the instructions awkwardly and I smiled and pulled him in quickly.

'Your servant, madam,' he stated. I nearly swooned, knowing he would play the game. In seconds he drew me to him and murmured: 'Madam, your pleasure is my desire.' I hope so!

My head on his shoulder, I closed my eyes, pressing my whole front against his manly torso, feeling the pads of muscle on his thighs. My fingers found their way into his shirt and his silky skin, I felt his hard cock nudging against me down there.

But he picked me off like some petal from a stem: 'Take it easy, we've got plenty of time, let me take a peek at you first.'

Glad to be admired, I submitted to his stare. It was as if he was tearing the dress off me with his eyes, and I lowered mine demurely. He fished out a scarf and waved it around my face, then blindfolded me. Hands were fluttering over me, fingers sliding the dress off my shoulders. Soon I had no idea where I was or who I was, I was just an object his tongue was flicking at, my naked bosom vulnerable to his devouring passion.

My dress slipped over my hips and onto the floor. He guided me to the cushions and laid me down. His expert tongue plundered my curves and flicked at my already-moist crevice. He hesitated and I groped for his head and made him come to rest with his mouth between my spread legs. I grew much hotter while he teased the entrance, licked it and fluttered inside. I was sailing on the good ship Pleasure. With a skipper half my age.

So far he had done what I asked in the letter, but I suddenly wanted to play with his prick. I moved forward and my lips searched for it, finding a fat mast all scorching and alive. But so tender. It was my turn to lick him and I was delighted to hear him making tiny simpering noises. I knew he was as lost as I was to reason and daily worries. We were both pent-up with energy, lusting for sex, knowing that the longer we explored the better the final liberation would be.

'One moment, madam,' he said with authority. 'I intend to carry out your instructions to the full. Squat down on the carpet.'

Blindfolded I obeyed as best I could, and I squatted there naked like a bitch on heat. I shivered as he came behind me and began running his hands all over my back. He pushed me onto all fours and lifted my bottom up so that I was exposed, in a dirty sort of way, indecently waiting for him. His tongue chivvied my two orifices, slipping upwards again and again. I had asked for it, and was still asking for it, but I could not help shaking. And at last his big mast pushed into my behind like a kind of rubber hosepipe and he went to and fro inside. This was pleasure enough, but he wanked me frantically too with his fingers, pulling at my twat, making me thrash my whole middle up and down in the savage sea of ecstasy! The climax was still to come, and at this point he took the blindfold off. He was as mad with lust as I was, that was clear from his gleaming eyes. We were calling to each other for communion, for the best that life could give, for eternity.

He came down onto me and the scales fell from our eyes. We were loving each other at that moment when our bodies, our sexes, our souls united.

Then he filled my void, completing the cosmic puzzle for me. We were out in space, bumping and jogging more and more violently, delirious with voluptuous and lascivious folly.

I felt the wave rise up within me, then a mighty sucking, and a tornado engulfed me.

We screamed as one as we came together.

Caroline

YES

Yes

Tomorrow, darling, it will be Thursday December 21st. All over the world it will be Thursday December 21st, and I love you with a clear golden love! I can at last tell you it is night.

The towns and villages no longer exist. The factories and the corridors in the Ministries are plunged in darkness. The pilot lights and streetlamps are dead. The power blackout of December 19th may continue, an authoritative source said today. In the country the farmers don't seem to be suffering from this temporary breakdown in electricity.

I have to admit I feel rather chilly. Because of emotions, the silence, the nights to come. All I can hear is an unknown volatile thing, a quiet plane high in the sky just out of Paris and heading for Los Angeles or some place like that.

Oh darling, I'm looking at your photo on the table. The room faces west, overlooking the vegetable garden, and I think I can hear people walking on the white gravel. Two men are scrunching up the path, one with a black blindfold over his eyes, the other talking to him. I could become blind with numbness.

I'll call the stables tomorrow around one.

One day we shall get married: 'Do you accept this man as your lawful wedded husband?' 'Yes!' I can at last utter the only word worth hearing. It will be an unquestionable yes.

'Phaedra is in every way a tragedy of enclosed speech, of restrained life.' She said yes! 'This trapped word is fascinated by its expansion.' I am trembling, and afterwards I shall ask you to cut my tongue off, and silently I shall ruminate that yes which cannot ever be taken back. She said yes with no echo.

A dog is rushing around outside the door. You are constantly pulling on the cigarette in the photo, with half-closed eyes deeply, probably a Rothman. I love your way of doing things and the things you read. I love your man's body, you and everything simultaneously.

The day has turned to night, and tomorrow we shall be Thursday. Oh my love, I do love you, without a word and without a tongue. I love you inside. Do you at least know what I look like in this cold December night? Have you imagined next winter or the winters farther away? I am inventing fears now. I shall look at the sun without you, it seems, only half seeing it. May my mouth on your eyes appease your sufferings, let my tears on your belly warm you inside! Darling, darling, I'm going to the bathroom, I'll be incredibly pure and white. I'll be smooth inside, intact and raw. I shall be spotless.

In secret and in silence I shall lick the last yes, the last word. I shall concentrate on chewing over the ultimate affirmation. I'll reach to the end of the yes. I'll marry your flesh, your fluid, your breath, your feet. I'll marry your skin. I shall be the perfect alliance, the golden ring of love. I'll be filled with unutterable words. I shall be hiding under your nails, on your back, completely part of your flesh's pale cells, cosy in the muscular fibres of your body. I'll be within you, your mother beauty, the heart caught up in love, the twin of love. I shall be twofold, two. And I shall be mixed in with your name. I'll be a fluffy ball of love, inside you and reciprocally yours. Never shall we be put asunder, and that means I'll be the yes of love.

The constant yes of love. The ever and ever yes of love. The body open for your love. I shall be the blue substance married to your name. In life and in death but one.

I shall be the absolute certainty of a hidden sense, the loving happy one. I'll be the indestructible kernel of a limitless love in orbit for century after century and circling at the sweet speed of my love for you. I'll be the unspeaking companion of the beyond, the bodily frame of love.

Annie Cohen

Solar Solitude

I feel myself sated with you. How sweet it is suddenly to feel that you are full of me too, even though I know nothing of it.

My finger poised between our lips, as if my mouth was now only your mouth.

How marvellous to speak to you with my body, as my head or fingers have never spoken so far, to speak to you with my body so much that my over-full head unexpectedly empties. And to welcome you in the dishevelled spot where my body has never yet committed itself so deeply, where my body lives again through the wordless language, and stirs beyond words; where my body really knows how to speak to you and answer you, you whose body throws me that crying silence; where my head no longer exists except through my body and my body through those words that don't mean anything. But you're there, yes you are there, and your presence calls out to me like a wild silence which, through solitude, has managed to discover the difficult rhythm of a nameless reply.

I need no words, I need no phrases. Simply your eyes when they yearn for me, your hands when they yearn for me, your body when it yearns for me.

There is nothing more I can tell you. I believe I really love you now. Take my breasts in your hands, come softly into my body and dance and keep dancing. Yes I truly believe I love you. But I won't actually say so, because I want to tell you physically, and if I don't know how to I'll learn, oh yes I'll learn!

I long for your flesh in my flesh, your life in my life. I long for us to be us.

You probably realize that I often look at myself in the mirror, to check on the face I mean to offer you. I often scrutinize the marks of suffering that have stayed on my lips to witness the pleasure I have had.

When you looked at me tonight I felt weak through loss of blood. It was as if my whole body left harbour like a ship for a long journey.

I can't forget how you bite my lips and I'm sure they are split open and bleeding, when you make love to me. How you kneel down behind me and touch my most private part, and then I venture to caress it and our two sets of fingers join and I start flowing so that we both get sticky. How I force my head back and try to kiss your mouth.

When we do that my body is tense and hard but my little tunnel yields to your ministrations. I wish I could express it better, but it's wonderful how you know about rousing me! I am mad about your body too, and I adore it.

It is wonderful, too, that I am familiar with your body, to the last detail now, and that there will still be something new to discover about it tomorrow. I feel faint just thinking about it.

You say my body is perfect, but when I sometimes refuse to let you do things it's because I want my body to be even more perfect. But believe me I love what you do, love it love it love it. When we seem to melt into each other and float – anywhere and nowhere, you know where!

Our bodies can speak, and you know I love what they say, more than I realize, more than you realize.

If only you were here seizing my body, I ache to have you right now, and to love you in return and kiss you all over.

On the phone you said: 'I kiss you on the thighs.' Nobody but you would know how to do it, because you know how much I like it on the thighs!

Isn't it exciting, learning about each others' bodies? Perhaps we may experience moments of emptiness, but ecstasy too, orgasms in every possible way.

You are already part of me, when you might be so distant. I see a picture of two trees representing our bodies, rain which is your juice mixing with mine, and also for the drops of perspiration wetting our skins. A red colour for your hair. And diamonds, reflecting the sun in the water and representing your eyes.

Suddenly as I write I remember the taste of your skin, incandescent skin, and I seemed to be just an enormous mouth kissing your body. When I feel like this I'd let you do anything with me. I'm imagining your skin against mine all the way down, thinking you will be coming in at any moment. My head is whirling, and I think of your head on mine just after you came inside me and you lost control completely.

Perhaps I seemed quiet to you when you left, but believe me my whole inside was shouting out, demanding your eyes and mouth and longing for delirious lightning flashes. At this instant I can feel the bitter-sweet wave building up in my inner ocean. I think of us naked and admiring each other.

How strong yet gentle was your mouth. No, I shan't read tonight, but will think about your kiss, quietly and nakedly enjoying it again with my eyes and body and everything.

If only I could have your whole body against me, our two beings joined. You've just left and I want you back already. Half asleep I murmur out to you, between reality and a dream, on the edge of another reality, drifting.

Don't say anything, just come back, and I will keep silent too. Let's press our mouths together, your penis in my vagina. Let your lips wander all over me finding secret parts, so that I have an orgasm not only on my own but with you as well and therefore together. I am a hot flame, and a woman too. Ah, I have found you again. Since you left I kept on thinking of your body and the way you move. Now I can feel your body inside me again, and want that kiss I refused you because of my nasty cold, want to love you, need your voice, your trunk and limbs, the salty tang of your skin.

I remember, remember, remember. Of course, you're not actually in me, but I am breathing quickly and so tempted to satisfy my mounting desire because I need you physically so awfully much.

It's amazing to think that I am free to love you always, at daybreak, twilight, in the middle of the night.

Suddenly I have a vivid picture of your handsome masterful look. The same one you had when you penetrated me last time. That too I can feel all over again, your stiff male sword ransacking me in there. Oh marvellous, it's just as if you were doing it to me again. My mouth must be twice its size, I feel so worked up, so juicy.

A few minutes ago I sat in the edge of my bed in my stockings and with those pretty shoes on. I crossed my legs elegantly and saw how silky the stockings were. What a pity you couldn't play with my legs. But perhaps you are at this moment thinking of them, getting excited because of my stockings, or my breasts or my face. Oh my dearest I'm going to die with wanting your penis inside me, the big bulbous end moving about inside my entrance, and your lust for me suddenly widening your eyes. I want you to lose control of yourself and forget me and walk over me as if I were a desert. How can I put it? I want to be your breath as you hold it just before you come. I'd like us together to dissolve utterly until we become a nothingness from world's light springs. I want to love you.

I love it when you take my head, ruffling my hair a bit, and push it backwards so that my lips are waiting for your kiss. How lovely, the idea of my face lost in your face! In fact I think it's the drifting of our merged bodies and minds that I want ultimately, the frenzy of our combined senses, the spreading of my own senses in the body of the world. An infinity of processes that make my eagerness for you grow huge. My rocky shore of senses must drift towards you alone, you who so perfectly contain the matter of the world for me. I want to feel you in the swaying tree, the smashing ocean, the silent rock. Even if sometimes there is no tree, sea or rock. From now on I simply want you to live in me, in a superb complexity and simplicity. It's something outside us both and I want it to drift from you to me and float off elsewhere. The movement must always be towards me and it must go back only to come to me again, just as the sea goes out and comes back in. That is what I mean by elsewhere, with me as the shore, with elsewhere making you even more real.

I am parched from my intense desire for your body, without you I am nothing, but with your body pressed into mine we can travel the world.

Everything seems to be shaking again at this moment, and I wonder which part of your body or mine or the world I must have touched to make it so stupendous, to invoke this carnal and topical feeling that is so abstract and poetic. I am dissolved in you, and I sense you as a fluid pervading my flesh. This I need desperately, your presence within me and outside. You know, I like talking about you to myself, it brings me on and I can almost see.

When we make love I prefer not to say anything much at first, letting my appetite guide me until my awakening gradually becomes almost entirely of the flesh. Silence is nice too, or just the odd word or two, and then when we have come and we are still united, we can chat with our bodies and minds together.

You're cute the way you say nothing as you push your thing inside me and thrust and rotate. So serious.

Oh, now I'm worked up again thinking about your mouth and pelvis pushing against me. For hours I've been trying to control the flood of sensations, goodness knows why, and they are all spilling out again, overwhelming me. I want you and it's making everything bright around me so that my body is evanescent as if we have just made love perfectly. Savouring this on my own is lovely too.

Follow me to the ends of my craziest desires, to the ends of my limbs and my life, follow me as we lose ourselves deeply in one another. I so wish that we could be more completely us and still different, because I'd like to brave dangers with you, throw myself into new nights and mornings with you.

Wasn't it super yesterday? At the moment I have only an obscure vision of your flesh, your pleasure, your eyes. It isn't that I want you entirely for myself, but I wish your body could be kept pure, remote and washed by my juice only. Back in my room where we made love so long ago, so recently, a week already ... I can't concentrate, do you think that if one of us comes the other can be made to climax as well by remote control? Do you think it's lots better, the most thrilling of all, when we do it in two places simultaneously?

For the time being I am just glowing with my desire to be part of you, and this urge in itself is driving me crazy. I asked you to bite my hand but what was I trying to achieve? Was I unable to accept your departure? Did I seek

to make your distance more real, nearer, less far away?
How the feelings ebb and flow away!

I didn't know where to put what I've just written, so on
my way to my bedroom I slipped it in my swimsuit so that
it is touching my little grotto, and we are again mouth-to-
mouth.

Sometimes I don't even want words, just your prick
poking me and laying me bare. I love the preliminaries
and they are never too long for me, so that the sweetest of
all acts is too fast.

I am wet-eyed, wet-mouthed and wet-faced this evening
because you are present in me and I implore your presence.
The surge I felt when you ran your hands over my
haunches as I stood drawing the curtains. Then I was
welded to you. I can see the stain we left on the sofa and
even that makes me tremble, thinking of your flesh in my
orifice, my lips swollen from your thick penis slipping
back and forth between them and feeling its delight. You
came right into my entrails.

Oh dearest one, I know my lips are swollen with the
same pleasure now, just as you saw them and rubbed
between them.

I have washed my panties, and even though I left them
to soak for ages with the other things, I can see there is still
a tiny sticky patch, sensual, gluey, unwilling to go away,
the remains of the gladness you brought on before I even
undressed for you.

There is ecstasy in my eyes as if someone has squeezed
the juice of three oranges into them. I remember that at
one point I felt the whole planet clinging to me and I let
myself go completely. Then we had flashes between our
faces, your mouth, eyes, nose, like the most sparkling
jewels and my whole frame jumped with electricity.

At dawn your hands found my bosom, and I looked
down on my breasts, as it were indifferently, watching
your hands playing with them.

I sailed on that ocean, pumping out juices and
thrashing about in ecstasy, welcoming your body and
spirit, yielding to you in all my female splendour and
naked before you. The feeling drifted from you to me, and

there was no longer either you nor I, and you became simply a machine thrusting again and again, jerking my body, bringing on a coma from purely carnal bliss.

Then it was my turn to caress you, and I did it expertly. Not that I had to concentrate, but because I felt myself thrown of a sudden into the act itself. Your hungry penis then became integral with my body as if I too was you and outside of you, myself and another, I was myself and more than myself.

I sometimes have visions of other faces, but it is yours that keeps impressing itself more than the others. I cannot say exactly why.

Simply longing for you again this evening is enough, it brings me relief, delights me. I am on my back, my legs bent and I feel you gently coming down on me, brushing my lips first of all so that I feel mine against yours so tenderly. I know I shall feel your penis at a particular moment, carefully trying to penetrate me. But I am in no hurry, liking this sensation that you are approaching, and I am trying to hold onto it.

Then suddenly I grab my notebook and write it down. As I write, oh wonderful, I feel that tingle of desire mounting again, I knew it would happen, I am letting my appetite have free rein and I soak myself in pleasure. There is only a little presence of mind left, and I know that I shall soon lose myself completely.

Ecstasy at last, you are here although you are absent. Tears are streaming down my cheeks, and they have diluted my mascara and it's running into my ears. I have heard it said that women cry when they haven't come. But they are not those sort of tears. I was delirious. No, it's simply that I love you. I am crying because I love you.

Sylvia Metz

A Sun In My Entrails

The water was marvellous.

It played with my legs and between my legs. I had never known such an intense and beauteous moment, and I prayed to the sea and the god who was looking at my nakedness to give me a child. A child made of sun and a dream.

Neijib was back there sitting on the beach, watching me moving and vaguely worried about me. He was handsome and the night flattered his appearance. Everything was silky and restful at this twilight hour. The water seeped inside my body like a man, softly, and for a second or two I thought I knew the happiness of a womb bearing a child.

Who would have persuaded me that this summer, under the superb Tunisian sky, love would be travelling with me, and that this man would be the bearer of my most fantastic dreams? Who could have convinced me that purity is still to be found in the heart of certain human beings? Who could have told me that I was to meet HIM?

He gave me necklaces every night and they smelled of jasmin, a lovely fragrance that will cling to my heart for ever.

Music from the nearby hotels serenaded us on our bed of fine sand. Sometimes it happened that we danced holding each other so closely, far from the gaze of the outside world. In due time our feet became too heavy and we slipped quietly onto the sand. The moon must have laughed at our awkwardness.

How long did the dream last? I can't remember any more. Time did not flee from us, it belonged to us, sharing our love and our fondlings. I recall only a moment, a sombre minute, in which hands were joined together, our chests constricted so that I was suffocating. We spoke phrases such as 'Why must we part?' and 'Never again' and 'Forget me' came and my enthusiasm was tarnished.

I had to leave that man behind me, and he grew smaller and smaller as I flew away. In the sun and on the sand I had to leave the imprint of our bodies behind me, strewn with faded flowers.

The moon will no longer mock us! And yet this evening, under my Paris sky, I fancy she is smiling at me. She is the accomplice of these early discomforts, the new-born weaknesses of my body which is now preparing to bear fruit. My breasts are swelling, and solitude is not happy.

Neijib, I believe the sea heard my appeal! A sun is growing in my entrails, one that will sweep away all frontiers, all wars, and will come and join you. A sun like you, handsome and pure.

Christine Corade

Puberty And The Rest

Being only 14 at the time, I could not understand why Carlos looked at me so intensely. How was I to know that he was practically burning my cotton panties off with his eyes?

The only reason I had any on at all was that my mother put me in short flimsy dresses, which I'd had for too long. It was summer and scorching hot and everyone seemed to be in the streets.

So when he looked at me in that special vacant way, I simply gazed back into his deep blue eyes, admiring the gold ring in one ear and thinking he must be a pirate. Then I would giggle and run off on my lanky legs tanned from the many hours playing outside.

Carlos was much bigger than I was, a Brazilian I was told, and I couldn't always understand what he was saying. But he was good-looking and I sometimes wished he would not look at me like that.

Sometimes he used to appear when I was on my own and would sit me on his knees, running his hands over my dress. One dress had buttons and he undid these to touch my little breasts. They were just starting to grow a bit and he used to chuckle when he did it. I liked it and he did it quite often.

One day he said: 'I'm going to see a friend of mine, would you like to come along?' and I said alright. But when we got to the flats we found nobody, although Carlos kept ringing the bell. He gave up and we stood there; it was fairly dark but his eyes had two specks of light in them. He put his hands on my shoulders and pushed me against the wall, then began kissing me on the cheeks, the neck and my eyes. He was whispering in Portuguese and I couldn't understand anything of course, but I told him to stop it as he was tickling me. With his right hand he undid his belt, and I was suddenly afraid because I'd heard such stories, and I giggled. But he pushed his tongue past my lips and right into my mouth, it was enormous and wiggled about. He was sort of snorting and put his hand under my frock and tugged at my panties, pulling them down to my knees, and then they fell right down. I said no he mustn't, and I wormed about. I said I was only 12 and someone was coming, but it wasn't true and he shoved his knee between my knees. The next thing I knew was his hot chopper hard against me and he was trying to lift me up. I felt dizzy and wanted him to stop, although I said to myself it wasn't my fault just because I'd agreed to come. I remember I wanted to cry then, and was about to scream when somebody started coming up the stairs.

He let me go, looked at me with a sort of pain in his eyes and hurriedly did his trousers up. I knew we had done something naughty and I pulled my knickers up quickly. He took me by the hand and we went outside. He bought me a Coca Cola, and said goodbye.

I was trembling, and I felt my cheeks burning. I kept thinking about it for a while and then forget all about it.

Then another summer, soon after my 16th birthday, I was at a cafe *terrasse* having an ice-cream. Why I was alone I can't remember, but there I was watching this boy going back and forth glancing sideways at me each time. It's the boys' job to make fools of themselves and he was doing it well. Naturally I did not show I was interested. He sat at a table nearby and I got up, going past him, licking my ice-cream, hoping it looked sensuous. Then I went and stood in front of him, my tongue slithering up over the ice. I asked him if he wanted a lick, and he said no, but blurted out that his name was Bruno. I extracted his age: 18. We teamed up for the afternoon, and he kept wooing me with his eyes, saying little, not smiling. It was rather boring really, but I rather liked bashful boys, not being too confident myself. He asked me for a date and we settled for that evening. As we played about with a couple of pizzas I was thinking he must have won a good conduct medal in sex education. Then he started saying 'I love you' now and again, which I thought peculiar. Even so he was rather sweet, and I decided he was as good as any other, so why not?

Although he lived some way away, I got him to invite me to his flat the next day. When I rang and the door opened, I found him rubbing the sleep out of his eyes. He just stood there in his white underpants with the bulge in the front. I turned my eyes away, but he said to come in and walked ahead of me. I liked his walk and his sunburned body, his cherry mouth.

We went into his room and the bed was in a mess. It was stuffy too because the temperature was rising fast despite the early hour. He kissed me on the mouth and I remained rigid, thinking that the idea was crumbling along with his legend. Awkwardly, I told him: 'I'm a virgin' and he said blearily: 'Well, I'd better not do it to you.' I had other ideas, and wouldn't let him get away with that, so I lay down on the bed, my skirt riding up. He began pawing me inexpertly, and to help him I swiftly took off my skirt. But I could not bring myself to touch him. He kissed me, then got on top, and I felt him hard through his pants. He fingered my knickers, loose-legged cami-knickers I wore specially, and made it easy for him to feel me with his fingers. He was so shy, and I simply lay there afraid to upset things, looking round at the dark room, the sun coming through the blind slats, listening to the traffic outside and the springs squeaking in the bed.

Eventually he plucked up the courage to remove my knickers and I lifted myself up, then he took his pants off and I closed my eyes. He parted my legs more and his thing pushed against my crack, being gentle as I had hoped. He fumbled it a bit but at last I felt his knob going in and he went further and further. I didn't feel moist but his probe slid in perfectly. I expected it to hurt, but he just went on getting deeper and deeper. I felt absolutely nothing, and was disappointed. He slid back and forth only twice and then came, muttering something, finally putting his whole weight on me and closing his eyes.

It was over. I was no longer a virgin. He opened his eyes and asked if I felt any pain. I detested him.

Even at 17 I had not really had 'it' with a man. I was so frustrated! Even though all sorts of men young and old used to ogle me in the streets or whistle after me. Everyone kept telling me I was pretty, meaning sexy, but they seemed like puppy dogs most of them, sniffing around.

I was invited to a party in super de luxe apartment with a large terrace-balcony and lots of beautiful people. It was fun, I danced and danced and felt at home because plenty of my friends were there. Plus this wonderful he-man whom I didn't know. We kept on meeting, swapping wisecracks and smiling. It seemed we were seeking each other out from the crowd. Well, as everyone knows, if you're in the mood it needs only a few cocktails and stuff, and your pulse starts quickening. He was attracted too, because somehow he managed to sit next to me on a sofa and he took my hands and played with my fingers and my palm with his own long slender fingers. I was so glad we were touching, and I was feeling alive for the first time in my life. His velvet eyes fluttered over me, and I loved my power to create a need in this gorgeous male. We stayed like that for a while, then he rose and as he pulled me up the room tilted! I had seen the empty balcony and knew he would take me onto it. Oh the sweet warm night! He took me in his arms and found my lips. I returned his kiss with everything I had. I gave myself up to the embrace, my whole body against his. All the tension flowed out of me: my shoulders, breasts, stomach, thighs. Incapable of the slightest resistance I let him push me to the balustrade, and he lifted my dress up past my stocking tops and then he placed a hand on my mound and sliding it down between my legs. His fingers touched the V of my panties which I knew were soaking and I was proud of it! People were glancing at us through the big window, but I didn't care. Leaking like a broken bowl, I desired him with a scalding heat. So much so that I undid his zip and plunged my hand into his pants, taking his taut stem and clenching it and feeling its stiffness. It was semi-limp to start with, but I made it swell, and my power to do this thrilled me. He sighed several times but said nothing, as if he was waiting for me to do something. Now his appendage was sticking out from his trousers straight at me and I raised one leg, clinging to his neck, then the other leg. I fell onto

49

him and he pierced me deeply, so deeply I completely lost all sense of propriety and clenched and unclenched my thigh muscles, making him penetrate me repeatedly. I slowed down and felt every stage of his passage within me, and each time I shook with the divine pleasure of it. We were blowing into each others' mouths, and we accelerated until at last he shifted somehow and gave an almighty thrust, emitting a high-pitched moan as he squeezed me tight with his powerful arms. I swear I felt his spunk pumping into me somewhere deep inside. My whole body heaved and I prickled right to the ends of my fingers and toes. It was the most intoxicating thing that had ever happened to me. I positively exploded!

We untangled ourselves and our combined fluids ran down my legs, but I was too weak to worry. A post-coital mist swam before my eyes, and I realized there was nobody looking out through the window, except just one young man who smiled at us.

My partner found a handkerchief and cleaned me up down there. I do believe I had another orgasm while he was doing it.

That was the first time I really made love. We did so as often as we could in the weeks that followed.

Emma Nhuel

My Neighbour

I set the alarm yesterday at 6 am. You have to make a choice: to sleep or make love. And I shall have years in which to sleep when I'm old and wrinkled.

In rubber boots, a large gardening apron round me, I went down the path hoeing up the weeds. There are very few left as I've done it so often lately. Please God let him be there this morning!

I saw him move behind the hedge, and my heart leapt. I must have him today, but I pretended to be busy. Then in a flash he had scrambled over the hedge, no easy thing because it's high and there are stinging nettles and scratchy bushes.

Pierre the neighbour. How awful to call him that! We do it so marvellously together, every time it's perfect, with both of us coming at the same time. It is a real miracle. And even when we chat and laugh it's fun. We are the perfect couple!

Afterwards I told him: 'Till tomorrow, my angel,' and the calves in the next field gaped at us.

Yesterday I planted myself in front of him looking into his delicious green eyes, not up at him for we are the same height. I told him: 'Pierre, my darling Pierre, I want to spent a whole night with you.' But he said: 'Be reasonable, they'd find out, we have to play it like this.' I was unhappy, but we went for a walk, being careful and scanning the landscape to left and right. Then it was cheerio until tomorrow, or at any rate Friday 7 am. It was to be a great year, totalling 12 months and 28 days. We got together as often as our families allowed it.

It all happened this way. I was exhausted and wanted to take things easy. But a whole avalanche of responsibilities fell upon me. 'Maman, I'm getting married next month; you'll look after everything won't you?' 'Could you possibly take my boy under your wing for a couple of weeks?' Nine hours' hard labour per day.

That was when Pierre became my lover, and the same

month I became a grandmother. Not that this worried me overmuch, but it's not easy to make up for lost time with a baby joggling on your arm!

'Do understand, darling, we can't fuck now with the baby wanting its bottle every five minutes.'

'All day long?'

'Just about!'

'Oh well, better luck tomorrow!'

And then there was the weather. Sunshine's wonderful but it also means the heavy work like haymaking, corn harvesting. The rain when it comes plasters your hair to your neck, all wet and dangling. Have you ever made love in nine inches of mud? Believe me it only happened in the films. We made love with the leaves of the trees over us, but it was damp afterwards – Wagnerian but wet! As to the snow, that's the worst of all, it leaves traces, and you have to clump about afterwards to confuse the meanies trying to collect evidence!

Through suffering we find love, they say. I used to love my warm old bed in my warm old house. I can be nostalgic but I've had some ambrosial times with my lover, enough to stir into my coffee for the rest of my life.

One day it was below freezing and we kept our sweaters on while we thrashed about in my flowered sheets. Three hours with his cock red and sore, but as firm as an iron bar!

There were tender moments when he arrived saying: 'I've had a shower, lick me, I'm immaculate and I'm all yours.' Or even more sentimental: 'I found a she kitten outside last night and took her in. I like caressing her, she has your eyes.'

Once he said: 'What a pity we never met when we were 20. You could have had your night of love then!'

I am genuinely happy with him, we go so well together. When he says: 'Oh you woman, you real little woman.' Well, I shriek with pleasure, until he tells me someone might hear.

Oh yes, we talked for ages. About his business, what he's been buying, his projects. I would lie there listening, leaning over to play with his tits, plaiting his hair, biting his sexual organs. And he would talk and laugh and enter me once more with the challenge: 'You can't get enough of it, always ready you are.'

But then someone I won't mention spoiled it all, and we don't laugh any more. An immense sadness is my companion now day by day; I cry into the soup I'm making, into the saucepans I'm washing up. I'm 20 years old again and the frustration is just dreadful.

Pierre, my sweet, you're unhappy now too. We have our responsibilities, and we are in our fifties.

Oh Pierre, my Pierre, there's so little time left. Let's have that last fling, we go so well together!

Jeanne-Marie Cris

GIRLFRIENDS

Pearl Of The Orient

I am the priestess of Kathmandu, the Mecca of Lesbos. For all my friends, I arrange evenings of pleasure.

On that Tuesday in November it was a butch evening with everyone in trousers and ties, in contrast with the previous evening when trousers were banned. I dislike jeans and suchlike and long for people in skirts and flower-like dresses: I hate the unisex fashion that turns ravishing girls into hoax boys. Anyway that night I found myself in a pair of wide trousers, a dickey, tails and plastered-down hair. I felt ill at ease in this disguise, because I never set out to ape men in order to seduce women.

Everyone seemed to be there in smoking jackets and bow-ties, laughing and trying to flirt in the mirrors of Kathmandu. Then came the moment for the show. To give it more punch I had engaged a couple of strippers who were resting between international tours. Lucky for us. They were tall, blonde and beautiful and I hoped they were well-proportioned. We were all rushing about in our dressing rooms, unable to watch each others' turns. But on the stairs I ran into one of the artistes, the girl I had made the arrangements with. Once again I was struck by the beauty of her eyes: the bright jade of a mottled effect. She had a high forehead, African hair-do and a multitude of blond tresses ending with coloured pearls. We had to squeeze between two lines of people and our bodies touched. She was quite naked. Instinctively I held on a little to her waist as I went up and she went down. Her skin was a little clammy, I noticed, and as was my habit I slipped my hands down from her hips to the bulge of her pelvis, just skimming her fleece because of the crowd, in the heat and excitement of the show. It was like silk. I had no time to mumble an excuse, for we lost sight of each other.

After the show I was back in my evening dress, still ill at ease and feeling like some penguin striding about on an ice-floe. The strippers were dressed, and 'my' girl was wearing a pale blue satin blouse and body-hugging white satin trousers. I conversed left and right, as people congratulated me on the show. The two girls were wonderful, very beautiful, plastic and erotic, I was told.

'How did you like the one with the plaits?' I said.

'Extraordinary, divine, amazing bodies, terrific breasts.' My lady customers were ecstatic.

I was hyped-up and hadn't the chance of admiring her since my hand had made contact with her skin. I went over to the strippers, who were in close conversation with the friends who had come with them. One of them seemed to be 'accompanied' but my blonde negress appeared to be unattached. I thanked them formally, said they had made all the difference, swapped a few polite phrases and went off to continue my role as hostess. I came across Dominique, my confidante and accomplice, a wicked creature who knows everything and misses nothing.

'You've made a conquest, darling,' she whispered.

'Oh, who might that be?' I said, as snooty as they come.

'Against the pillar there.'

Naturally I was curious and, to my astonishment, I found she was referring to 'my' girl, Vanessa.

'You're joking,' I said. 'In this outfit?'

'Make no mistake,' Dominique urged. 'She can't keep her eyes off you.'

I flushed: 'You really think so?'

It so happened that my love affairs were going wrong at that moment, I was run-down, heading for a break-up. Which meant I was available, ready to go hunting again.

'Of course I'm right, I never make a mistake and you know it,' Dominique went on. She, my *eminence grise* and tempter, kept on murmuring encouragement, reassuring me, telling me it was a dead certainty. But whether I had the pluck to verify her assertions was another matter, especially dressed as I was. And to think that when I was a little girl I was so disappointed not to be a boy, found women so pretty and wanted to be a womanizer like papa! Tonight I was dressed exactly like papa but I had never been so scared, so little sure of myself. I would never be able to charm the girl.

And yet I moved off towards her, and like some champagne Charlie put one hand on the pillar either side of her. She stood facing me, in my power as it were.

'I'm afraid I don't look my best in this monkey suit, but I'd like a dance with you.'

And she smiled, her sparkling teeth in lovely red gums, a little vixen with generous fleshy lips.

'I'd love to.'

I took her a few steps, finding her supple, light, yielding. her body nestled in my arms, and we danced close saying nothing. I was rocking her in my arms, and we made not a single false step, seeming to swim among the female couples awaying around us. She held on to me tightly, and after a while her hands slowly crept round my neck, her fingernails softly tracing lines there. She had given me the come-on and I drew apart from her. We exchanged smiles of complicity, and I took her by the hand.

'Let's have a drink of something.'

'I'm afraid I never drink.'

'You're right, I'm sure. It's not necessary, there are other ways of being intoxicated.'

The flower-seller went by at that moment and I took a rose and gave it to Vanessa. She accepted it, bit the petals with her soft lips and smiled at me. She resumed her position against the pillar, and I buzzed around her like a lost bumble-bee. I went off and then came back to her, undecided about the next step, watching her anxiously. She refused to dance with another woman.

Dominique sidled up to me: 'I've been watching, you've made it.'

I still had doubts, and in any case I'm not keen on one night stands. I like to feel a fondness for a girl before making love to her, to serenade her before I start climbing over the balcony. But I had to act fast, because Vanessa and her colleague were leaving tomorrow, and I may never see her again. The contact with her body, pressing against her, had thrown me off balance, and I was seized with a yearning for this compliant flower of a girl – at once! I decided it was now or never, I must be bold.

'Where are you spending the night?'

'With our friends.'

'Do you have to? Surely they won't mind if you give them the slip.'

'But we're flying to Germany tomorrow.'

'When exactly?'

'I don't really know.'

'Find out, I'm kidnapping you. Come home with me and I'll bring you back tomorrow, I promise.'

She played hard to get, but I persisted, arguing to myself that I had plunged in at the deep end and could not funk it now. I knew she was tempted, and was simply being coy for appearances.

I said: 'You know you'll come, and you know I know. Don't let's waste a moment more. Why lose the few hours ahead of us?' I was pleading, catching her unawares, luring her, charming her. My innards contracted when she gave in, slinking over to her colleague, leaning over a table to speak to her. Oh that bottom! They kept on a bit about the venue and the time next day. And then Vanessa came back with a ravishing smile on her face. She was mine for the rest of the night!

I whispered a goodnight to Dominique and attempted a discreet exit with my new-found playmate, but people tittered and said goodnight excessively loudly. My car was just outside, and for once it was not raining. Paris was deserted, slumbering as it is every night when I drive home. I went along the Seine, once again enjoying the quiet of the river with the barges alongside. I adore the Seine's serenity, the dark hush through the city centre that never fails to clear my head of fumes and metallic music. Besides, a river is always romantic in itself, and this one sends ripples through me as I imagine myself holding the waist of a pretty girl while we gaze down into the water.

The same visceral urge clutched at me that night, but I controlled myself, merely allowing my hand to stray to Vanessa's knee and sliding it higher over the firm flesh within her skintight trousers. She was warm, and I sensed that a false move on my part would have her kicking and biting. We said hardly a thing, for we had nothing in common that we knew of, simply this physical attraction that would fade with the dawn, when I had stormed her Bastille!

I led her into my place by the hand, putting on just one lamp, not wishing to spoil the magic. I was delighted to note that Vanessa kept away from it, and so did I. As every night, I glanced out over the Seine, which had long been the backcloth to my dreams and my loves, and then led my new friend to the sliding glass door.

'Lovely, isn't it?' I ventured.

She said nothing and my brain stem jammed tight. She was waiting passively, perhaps changing her mind. Between a man and a woman, there is no argument about who makes the first move, the code has been established for centuries, the first two minutes of the screenplay are easy to understand. Between two women it's the *commedia dell'arte*, neither daring to take the initiative, neither prepared to submit. A woman can be Juliet tonight and Romeo the next. This time it was clearly my role to move into battle, for the citadel was already waving the white flag!

What am I saying? I hate the brute rush, it's twice as nice when it's slow. Some may prefer to rape or be raped, crying out rude words, behaving like raunchy sows – especially women who are in the public eye most of the time, they like to wallow in muck. But I like half-tone pictures, delicate movements like lace, giggles that end in embarrassed smiles, tiny touchings, movements that hold promise. I took Vanessa in my arms and we kissed. She responded passionately, and then I pressed harder against her two fleshy cushions, forcing her mouth open with my tongue, breathing in her erotic fragrance. Standing together, we melted into a single lascivious entity – hot, vibrating and heady. Already I was imagining her pouting sex, but I forced myself to hold back. It's twice as nice when it's slow!

Thanking my luck at that moment, glad I was as I was, I began undressing Vanessa, and she tackled my suit.

'This is the first time I have actually struggled with a

man's suit,' she breathed.

'Wait till you get inside. Keep going, *cherchez la femme!*'

We sort of hummed together, and made squeaking noises like a pair of convent girls in the changing room. Then I had her naked and my palms were sliding over her fine-grained skin, an almost Asian skin whose warmth was driving me crazy. In adoration, I lightly massaged her exquisite contours, lifting her breasts, her saucy little bottom, ruffling her hair a little. She had a compact bosom, round breasts that scarcely fell, and the tiniest pink nipples I had ever seen. These last I fingered and squeezed and within seconds they became stiff. I could not resist twisting them, and I saw that it hurt her. Still she said nothing, and we sat for a moment on the divan. Vanessa seemed to undulate as she walked from the window and I was already licking my lips at the thought of what I would be doing to her within minutes. Short of a catastrophe, she was at my mercy, I could do what I liked with her!

We exchanged more honey kisses, our lips double their normal size, while our fingers explored each other and massaged each other.

Emitting hardly audible noises to fill the silence, she allowed me to spreadeagle her on the bed, and I was at last able to stare openly at her sex. Kneeling between her feet, I gaped at her soft mossy bank, her fern-covered grotto, the fat little lips in the undergrowth, with a juicy pearl slowly easing itself out between the crack, even as I looked. I saw that she had closed her eyes and I homed in on her, meaning to pander to her narcissism.

In a single movement I grabbed her haunches and lowered my open mouth onto her thatch, kissing and licking and sucking until she started flowing abundantly. She lifted her knees, then her feet, giving me full access to her sopping crack. I pushed my tongue inside, my mouth wide open. I let my tongue go loose and licked her repeatedly from anus to clitoris. I inserted my tongue and worried her button with my nose. I slobbered until the spittle was cold on my chin. My mouth journeyed from her knees to her navel and then attacked her once more until every nerve-end was alive and screeching. The more frantic I became the more passive she tried to be, but I went on until I forced her to jolt and squirm. She was my violin, my viola, my cello, my harp, my zither, my big-bellied guitar – a whole orchestra! As I tugged at her bottom, the masive bronze dune of her belly rose and fell and she cried out, my Vanessa pleaded for more. She became a tempest, a sea with 30 foot waves thick with white surf. She was a symphony and I was conducting her!

I completely lost my head and at that moment I loved her. Never before had I found a woman so like myself. So much so that I seemed to be making love to myself as I was 30 years earlier, when I had been the passive one, heaving and gasping as she was, drunk, captivated, bewitched. It was too much, and I suddenly came up and threw myself down upon her, rubbing against her whole body, our vulvas squashing together, our legs entwined, twisting an arching, spreading and clenching. I was making love to Vanessa and to myself aged 20. We were desire made flesh, ardent, giving ourselves to each other. Utterly!

Professionally, Vanessa and her colleague had mimed the act of love between two women, on stage. But this time she was letting me do it with her in genuine pleasure, with no audience, just for the physical thrill. Perhaps she was seeing me as her audience. Perhaps to her one woman lusting for her was worth a packed auditorium.

We did everything together, absolutely everything, having orgasm after orgasm, until we were exhausted and the cold first light of the winter's new day forced its way through the clouds. A couple of pigeons made fruity noises on the ledge outside.

'I'm famished,' said my guest after we had dozed for some minutes. And we breakfasted on fruit and milk. She told me she was a vegetarian, and I realized I was indifferent to her tastes, her future. She cared not one damn about mine either. We had simply spent a night in our own little orgy, after a chance meeting. We both knew what we wanted, and it was the knowledge that we may never do it again that had thrown us into our frenzied efforts, had set us on fire, aware that we had to squeeze into one stretch of a few hours the experiences that others enjoyed over years.

I dropped her outside Le Flore restaurant, we smiled and hugged each other a last time.

'Next time you're in Paris ...'

'Yes, of course ...'

Still undulating, she eased herself out of the car, looking somewhat incongruous in her shiny satin things.

She gave the door a slam, leaned through the window and her eyes sparkled: 'Thanks again for a delicious evening!'

I laughed nervously, as the lights changed to green. We shook hands and I roared off, still in a state of zero gravity. We had parted satisfied and joyfully, no cloud had insinuated itself between us from start to finish. It had been a perfect dream. I had made love with many women, but none of these adventures had left me so lighthearted, walking on air.

Hidden in the crumpled sheets, where we had bounced and flung ourselves about, I found a small red pearl from Vanessa's hair. I played with it for a while between my fingers, seeing it as a droplet of blood, a bead that was left of a dream.

I have it still, all that remains of Vanessa apart from the memory. A pure pearl of the Orient from the necklace of our passion.

Elula Perrin

Leather And Velvet

I was staring at the carpet thinking of her in the bathroom, wiping off her make-up, getting ready.

I was shivering, partly from apprehension and partly because I was face-down on the sofa wearing only my velvet jacket and nothing below. I threw dice, and chewed almonds, sliding my tongue over my lips to collect the bits. I waited.

Then I heard her finish, I looked up and she was in the doorway, a look of cupidity on her face. Annie had removed every trace of make-up, and her hard round face with its jutting sadistic chin looked at me under her close-cropped hair henna-ed the night before. I lowered my eyes meekly, though not before I had taken in her brown pubic triangle, dark red nail varnish, her ample bosom and rotund haunches.

Annie stood for a moment near the sofa, wearing only her bronze leather boots with their sweet almost sickly smell that caught me in the throat.

The toe of one boot advanced under my chin and imperiously flipped it up, forcing me to look at her directly. She jerked her head and I obediently kissed the leather toe. She turned and I got up without a word, following her to the room across the thick carpeting, watching the boot heels dig in, her rump swaying and revealing some hair between her legs.

We reached the bedside and she made a token adjustment to the fawn velvet jacket I had on, bearing a white carnation. Then she flung back the bedclothes and lay back on the bed in her boots, using the heels to kick the clothes right to the end. Wordlessly I covered her body with mine, moving so that our labia met and spread, then oscillating so that my little button fenced with her fat clit. My velvet jacket sides flapped against our naked sides, just as she liked it, and her boot heels dug into my ankles so that I sobbed. We continued, the leather made its familiar voluminous floppy noise and the velvet whispered in its secret way, the jacket lining of silk sizzled too. A triple excitement. Annie stopped me for a moment and pinched her breasts in turn so that the now-stiff nipples caressed the carnation in turn. I took the carnation and laid it on her wet cunt that was gaping like a wound, then resumed my position pushing against her sex again and again until my backbone hurt. I brought her to her climax, her boots scraping against my legs and digging in harder. We swapped positions after that and she took the sopping carnation from my own sex and ate the petals one by one. We disentangled ourselves, and she slowly removed my velvet jacket.

Then she went over to the coat-rack and took hold of the whip. It had an embroidered handle and was in bronze leather, the whip itself half an inch thick.

Christine Delcourt

Trip To Portugal

I was preparing my psychiatry thesis, and wanted nothing so much that April as to dash off to Portugal with practically no luggage, and perhaps tour some of that lovely country by bike.

Who can explain holiday choices? Anyhow I was chatting about it to some students, and a girl suddenly said: 'I'd love to see Portugal too. We could use my car.' I said, 'Why ever not?' and promptly forgot about the whole thing. July saw the completion of my thesis, and I changed my mind, wanting to go to Brittany instead.

So I was irritated as much as surprised when she took me up on our earlier agreement. I paused awkwardly, looking at the phone receiver, not daring to tell her the Portuguese idea was just a passing fad because I'd heard a catchy tune of the radio.

Lost for arguments, I gave in and reluctantly found myself sharing the drive down the Autoroute A 6 in her *deux-chevaux*. Someone had told me she loved poetry and, as I did too, it finally decided me.

She was a curious girl, incomplete in some way, too young for anyone to tell whether she would turn ugly or attractive. Of course it's largely up to oneself, but a girl who knew her told me she was intelligent and revealed finesse behind her scruffiness, but 'needs a man to pull her together.'

Scruffy she certainly was. I had noticed her unstitched hem, her skirts held together with pins, and nobody could ignore her abundant mousy hair enclosing her face like an inverted bird's nest! She wore thick-lens glasses but when she took them off and rubbed them with a handful of skirt, a pair of delicate blue eyes looked out, and you began to notice other things: her nicely-shaped slender nose, her well-contoured mouth that any model-girl would have been satisfied with. Her chum was right, a man would have got her under control. But I had a feeling that no male mouth had approached those lips so far. Would they ever?

Then there was her room, which I went to once or twice before we set out. There were books and clothes dumped anywhere, and scores of seemingly empty face cream jars and other beauty aids. She could never have afforded them on her allowance, and in any case she hardly used any make-up, just powder and a sometime over-garish lipstick. What had happened to all the cream?

So off we went. We were not far into Portugal when she went into a fit of uncontrollable anger because a bunch of kids were dirtying the car with their sticky hands. I started giggling, and she rounded on me. I shrugged it off, but other things puzzled me. Before lunch I would knock on her room door, and she would let me in with haggard eyes and a generally dishevelled appearance. No jars of cream on this trip. I noticed too that she drank heavily: aperitif, wine and liqueur; I had to keep up with her as best I could, for politeness. And as we drove along she always seemed to be saying: 'I could do with a beer.' It never occurred to me that she might be an alcoholic, as I never dreamed of 'examining' friends and acquaintances, psychiatry being strictly a business affair. It was all rather tense. I am not the type who reacts to nervy people by making it worse, especially on holiday, and yet I was grateful we had our own rooms and at times different hotels, depending on what was available. She could be quite disagreeable, as when on one occasion she put a parcel on the car hood, deliberately crushing an insect because it was messing the paintwork. I found her smell rather off-putting, although intriguing. A sad grey girl.

She was so snappy all the time, and we were both very tired on the way back to Paris. We got as far as Angouleme and all the hotels were full.

And then just after midnight we finally found a place with one vacant room with a double bed. Exhausted we undressed, she smiling in an indirect way that I was tempted to judge neurotic. We put the light out, and less than a minute later she began weeping and when I asked what was the matter she flung herself into my arms. In a flash I realized how blind I had been.

And then ...

Helene Markich

But For David Hamilton ...

It was a revelation for me, the film *Bilitis*, when I saw it for the first time. I was not among the *cognoscenti*, and since I was 15 had simply been a fan of David Hamilton, whose soft wispy photos are universally acclaimed. In fact for some time I had had a poster of the film over my bed called *Comme Deux Soeurs* showing, in that characteristic diffused halo of light, a dreamy woman sitting in a romantic wicker chair. Everyone knows the picture. An adolescent girl, Bilitis of course, knelt with her head on the older woman's lap, and around them were large plants emerging from all over the place. The two figures are shown through some French windows, which gives the viewer a feeling of intimacy.

I went to see the film on my own. The extracts from future films went by, and then the ads, and then the lights went up and the chocolate and nuts lady wandered about. I looked around, of course, noticing how people were dressed mainly, and then the lights dimmed and went out. I nestled down, careful to keep my sling-bag on my lap.

The artistic quality of the film, the utter beauty of the first few feet, overwhelmed me. Splendour, softness, brightness, magnificence – I still can't describe it. And the music! So melancholy, so absolutely right for the mood Bilitis was in at that moment when we saw her for the first time. She had been on holiday and her loves had left her with a radiant happiness tinged with a sour taste. How I understood what she was feeling!

Then we got to the sequence when Bilitis and Melissa, the older woman, made love. Bilitis, not yet a mature woman, struggled to keep her balance as every day produced its new sensual impressions and experiences. I was rather embarrassed to start with, as no doubt others were but I didn't think of that, simply thanking my lucky stars we were in the dark. But you know how it is with a good film, you forget everything and I was wafted heavenwards by the sheer loveliness of the screenplay, the

70

wonder of those smooth satin naked bodies in the dim light, the sweet affection in the gestures between Melissa and Bilitis, and the tenderness of their facial expressions. There was not the least sign of brutality, vulgarity or pornography, just an enchanting sweetness that took me completely out of myself.

At the end I could not move, I just stayed there in my seat still seeing the thrilling pictures, hypnotized by the music that was so entirely right for the film. It was one of the deepest experiences I had ever had.

That film transformed my life. From then on, I found I was looking at certain kinds of women in a totally new way. And inevitably I fell in love with one. I will not reveal her name or the circumstances. Suffice to say that it began platonically with no hint of physical desire. I would simply admire her as she walked along, spoke, made gestures. And then it dawned on me that I actually desired her, wanted to touch her body, so harmonious to my eye, so softly curved. She had bronze shiny eye shadow and used black khol. I wanted to enter into her eyes, breathe in her velvety golden skin, run my hands over her, exchange little kisses with her, feel her against me, to close my eyes in her embrace and forget everything.

If only we could have got through to each other, I would have stuck with her for ever. Alas, it could only be a dream, and I had to admit that the best I could hope for was to listen to her gentle voice, swoon secretly every time her gaze came my way, cat-like and with an Oriental hint to it. I would have done anything in this world for her, but of course she had no idea of the 'crush' I had for her. I gave no sign of what I was going through, at least I don't think so, and at times I was really rather ashamed at actually yearning for another woman. Although she seemed to like me and gaily chatted with me, even going out of her way to approach me, I never supposed that by pure coincidence she was responding to my longing for her.

Then I lost touch for a while, catching a glimpse of her very occasionally, but she did not notice me. I still felt the same about her, finding her more beautiful each time, a queen, a goddess from Olympia, above us common mortals. She was highly intelligent too, and used her brains wisely in her studies, then in the job she had afterwards, rising to a fairly senior position in her firm.

It occurred to me that, if she really was that intelligent, she would be sensitive too, and perceive my disarray. If she happens to come across these lines, she might possibly recognize herself. However that may be, I know I shall love her always, shall be aware of her constantly as I am aware of myself, that although we are physically apart our souls will meet in the after-life. We live far apart but for me we are together through thick and thin. She is around me all the time, I can sense her presence. She will never escape me whatever the distance between us.

She is my diamond, throwing off a thousand tiny fires and shining eternally in the void. I am a little ray of light caught inside the heart of that precious stone, in the centre of her heart.

Often I imagine we are alone, just the two of us. Voluptuous whorls of inebriating ambergris and sandal-wood swim around us, and I seem to be floating in the air like a soap bubble. As one, we ascend in a pink perfumed cloud, away from all the violence and aggression on the earth, both wearing feather-light transparent togas so that I can see her honey-coloured skin which is velvet to the touch and gives off a delicate vanilla fragrance. She turns gracefully and smiles at me, and I look back not daring to move a finger. Her mere presence causes me to weaken at the knees, but she takes me to her and exerts the slightest of pressures on my back, enveloping me. I nuzzle into her firm springy breasts and roll my head in those exquisite orbs, as she gently massages my back and the nape of my neck. Her countenance hides everything else and I can see her warm lips glide past and plant a kiss on my neck. Her fingertips caress my shoulders.

Crushed against her lovely white breasts, my own made flat against hers, I can feel her heart beating with vigour and love, her hot blood careering through her brain, a torrent that makes her whole body throb. I want it to last for ever. But I desire her too, and my breathing becomes

72

hesitant, more anxious as my parched lips seek out the lowest point of her neck. I am completely subjugated, bewitched, and I lift my arms, close them round her neck, and we melt in a passionate and sensual kiss. Now I feel her cool slim white hand lifting my chin so that we look directly into each others' eyes, I am lost in the black and dilated pupils of the woman I love, and I think I am going to faint.

Clinging to each other, we sink onto a rich thick carpet, opulently white, and she gradually removes my flimsy toga and my whole torso prickles with delight and anticipation; the garment rustles over my abdomen, my mound, my thighs and knees, tickling my toes. I am soaked, and a violent heat burns from somewhere in my pelvic basin, it devours my entrails, and when she lays her hand lightly on my panting belly I fear I shall suffocate. I can keep still no longer and I feverishly tug at her garment, undressing her, exposing her superb body in its entirety, my hand trembling as I slip the thin material down from her fleece. All my inhibitions have gone and I have only one intention now: to obtain pleasure from her body. Ardently I bestow moist kisses on her front, her neck, her thighs and under her breasts, finally nipping the points of her breasts, making them plead for more.

A more urgent need surges through my loins, I go over her and plunge into her torso, moving my legs over hers. But we part, for we know both of us that the erotic foreplay is over and that we are now ready for the explicit sexual joys we have so far not dared to indulge in. She moves a hand between my legs, and her polished nails find their way into my quim, which I can feel swelling and opening like a flower. She caresses me and quickly vibrates my clitoris, finally inserting her long middle finger, then another pushing them deep inside me. Now she masturbates me in long firm thrusts, slowly rising and withdrawing, sending waves of pleasure through me with each stroke, until with each rise and fall of her fingers I jerk and push myself against her hand. A stream of juice floods through me and I am a huge volcano spilling out lava. I let out a cry and shut my eyes tight as an almighty pain sears up my vagina, and I can see a constellation bursting in my head! As I lie gasping, blowing uncontrollably through my mouth, she withdraws completely, leaving me to recover. I can hardly get my breath for a minute, and then the loveliest glow fills my body from tip to toe. I can feel sweat on my forehead, and I look down and observe my salmon pink skin, still vibrating with love. With a huge sigh I tell her: 'I love you,' and she kisses me lightly. Then comes her own husky declaration: 'I love you.' I drift off on a cloud of happiness, we exchange smiles, tender looks and cling to each other.

I lean over and kiss her lovingly on her swollen mouth, and our tongues flirt for a while. There is a pleading in her eyes, and I descend to her pelvic mound, gliding my mouth over the silky surface, and down to her fleece, where I breathe in her intimate perfume. With infinite care I part her vulva, and she spreads her legs. She takes my hand and guides it where she needs it, then lets it go. Inch by inch I advance within her sheath, which grows wider, and I begin rubbing her bud. Her torso seems to spread on the carpet, her bosom rises and falls, the orbs ballooning and their veins standing out. She is giving herself up to me, trusting me, gulping for air. Soon my rubbing brings her to a threshold and she can't stop herself bucking to meet my rhythm. Her knees come up and I know she wishes my fingers were twice their size, she wants me to do it harder and harder. And then she screams and lifts her torso off the ground, jogging frantically with her orgasm. Her rasps and moans are her hymn to the god Eros!

I can do no more for her, and she emerges from her ecstasy with my hands caressing her all over. We shift to a sideways position, clutching at each other, digging our nails in, tears of joy pouring down our cheeks and into our mouths. A luscious longing salty kiss seals our eternal love.

I see her often, the woman I love. We wander through a fairyland that must be the Mytilene, formerly Lesbos. The sapphire night envelops us thickly, taking us under its wing, and we stroll along a beach of golden sand, the waves lapping at the edge. The air is sultry and a light breeze sings in our ears. We approach a natural little harbour with rocks all around, and stay there a moment breathing in the air laden with iodine and the pungent seeweed smell. There is a small boat in the cove and we get into it, rowing off in the direction of the honey-coloured moon. We land on another beach, jump out, and she leads me by the hand to a half-concealed cave. Eerie music surrounds us and I am afraid to enter the cave, but she tugs at me. We go through a long tunnel and emerge into a lighted clearing where a feast is going on. Men and women in the scantiest of clothing are eating and drinking and laughing. Some of them are in groups of three, four or five, making love together. Others are in pairs copulating in every imaginable position. My attention is caught by a handsome couple, the man seated and the woman straddled across him, her fleshy bottom bouncing up and down between his massive thighs. They have their arms about each other and their eyes are wide as they near the climax of their pleasure. They are positively leering at each other. But suddenly the woman gets up, then goes down on him again, guiding his penis carefully into her quim. She moves back and forth and round and round lasciviously. She emits little squeaks as she goes faster and then the man roars like a bull. They come simultaneously and frenetically pull at each other, finally falling apart and collapsing onto the humid moss, their legs splayed to the utmost and their raw, empurpled genitalia exposed to view.

The two of us exchange smiles. We had comparable pleasure not long ago, intenser still perhaps. But we have no time to reflect, because a luxuriously-fleshed woman approaches us, her eyes shining and her heavy breasts swaying with a diamond-necklace between them, accentuating the lubricious effect.

'Welcome to our island,' she croons, beckoning us to follow her. The woman's feet scarcely touch the ground and tiny bells tinkle round her ankles. We too are floating like dragonflies. She takes us into a resplendent palace with walls of pink marble encrusted with pearls and rare precious stones forming arabesques and ribbonwork of intricate design. We pass through a solid gold door, and our guide leads us through a labyrinth of corridors as far as the throne of the High Priestess Sappho.

Sappho is infinitely beautiful, a sight to behold, her dull gold tresses falling to her breasts, her skin milky white and translucent. We kneel before her and she gives us her blessing. A dove flutters in through an open window, a white ribbon in its beak. The bird describes circles above our heads, then descends to twice the immaculately clean ribbon round us. Sappho smiles kindly, her magnificent emerald eyes giving off a mysterious supernatural brilliance. She has a perfect bone structure, regular features made incandescent from some inner light.

'I declare you united evermore,' she pronounces with deep solemnity in her voice of bronze.

Our souls are thus locked together for eternity, and no power in the cosmos can separate us. Our love is indestructible. Our wild passion has been consecrated, we are divinely wed for always. No storm or enemy can divide us, however strong they may be. We shall never know torment, nor fear, nor any other imperfect sentiment known to humankind.

Sephora

My Teacher

It was at boarding school, Blanche. I was a fresh 17 and you were 26. How lucky you gave me private lessons. Or was it intentional?

One evening you told me to come to your room, where you gave me a drink and locked the door. Then you sat on the edge of the bed, and pulled me brusquely to you. I remember I wanted to hit you but my fists failed to make contact, for your strong hands were holding my wrists. I thought how like a man you were, with broad shoulders and a heroic profile. It needed that little struggle to make me realize I was fond of you.

I admitted defeat and you ran your hands over my body, took my uniform off, then my underclothes. You looked at my naked frame with a lustre in your eyes. I had cotton wool flowing through my veins at that moment, and we were both breathing deeply as I clung to you and your arms folded round me. Your musky smell made me quite heady and I could hardly get my breath, excited at this completely new experience that was happening to me. I grew mellow and wanted you, to have you swimming in my waters. I was fascinated by your navel, I remember, your two white breasts shaped like melons and with their sugary fragrance.

Trembling at this first-ever sexual contact with an adult, I gladly placed my own small apples against you and you lay back while I wiggled my nipples around yours and you kissed me on and around my mouth. Before long our tongues were playing and you craftily took advantage of my confusion to push your fingers into my opening. You made me bigger down there. Gradually, and incredibly, you got all five fingers in and forced them into me. My vagina seemed to be bleeding, and the pain was delicious, the wickedness and secrecy intoxicating. As my desire mounted I grew bold and did it for you, exploring your tunnel, fascinated at your wanton abandon and your staring eyes.

We got on our knees and pleasured each other like mad things, our middles surging back and forth until we both came with little cries. Our bosoms shook like jellies and we tucked our heads down in our paroxysm. Afterwards you collected our juices and put your wet fingers on my mouth so that I could taste the saltiness.

You wanted to go on. You lay back and told me to put my head between yours legs, saying 'do as you are told'. As I did so you splayed your legs right open, vulgarly, and I roused you again with my grovelling mouth, wanting to go inside you. My face streamed with your fluid.

I said I must go and you prevented me. With puffed lips you kissed me to sleep. In the early morning I stole out.

For months, night after night, we enjoyed ourselves, and got rings under our eyes.

During the day you were Madame and I called you 'vous' in the formal way. You were my respected teacher, but at night I was your slave and mistress.

Agnes

SEX COCKTAILS

Long Live Love

He was standing legs apart on the main steps, frowning like Napoleon. I had slipped out of bed before he woke.

'And where do you think *you've* been?' he demanded. 'You went out without permission, and you know the punishment for that. And in a skirt!' I shifted uneasily from one leg to the other. 'I have told you time and again you must wear shorts when you leave the house. Take that skirt off.' I did so. 'Furthermore, I have strictly forbidden you to wear underclothes. Take them off.' I stepped out of them. 'Now you will walk round the entire grounds with nothing on. Let's see what a little discipline will make of you.'

I walked round the perimeter, setting off without a word, shivering with the cold and with trepidation. He followed me, hitting me with his riding whip hard, so that I jumped.

'Not high enough!' he declared, as the whip cut across my bottom, more painfully than before.

I must have had a score of stripes all over my back when we reached the steps again, and I could feel some blood dripping down the cheeks of my behind.

He gave a nasty chuckle and said: 'Spread your legs.' I hesitated, for this was the worst of all. Then I went up two steps and did what he ordered. The whip stung my sex from below, and the end flicked my bottom.

He sent me in, my body stinging with pain. Then he gave me a final stroke across the front, hurting my breasts terribly.

We went into the bathroom, where he soaped and rinsed me for a long time, telling me how he loved me. He made me lie on the rug beside the bath and made love to me, then told me to get on all fours. Placing a towel under my neck he pulled my head back so that my rear ballooned up, and penetrated my back passage. Next we were in the bath together, sitting facing each other. I rested my legs on the sides and he took the thing off the shower and put it in my anus, squirting hot and cold water in me. My husband ordered me to lie on my back on the table in the bathroom, and I writhed in pain so that I had to rub my abdomen. Finally I had my first orgasm so far.

He hadn't finished with me yet. He placed tiny cones on my breasts, with the nipples poking through holes, then gave me an injection in each breast as part of a treatment to make them large. It was very painful, and he gave me another injection next to my navel to reduce the flesh on my front, so he said. Then he made love to me again.

I had to clean everything up afterwards, and then went out to do some shopping, and call in at the bank.

When I got back, he said he was surprised to see me in a mini-skirt, and a very close-fitting one at that. He put his hand under it and said it was lucky for me I had nothing on underneath.

My husband stood by as I unloaded the shopping onto the kitchen table. He picked out a rather big carrot and spun me round with an unkind clasp at my arm, then forced me to bend over by grabbing at my neck, finally shoving the carrot into my back passage. I asked him to take it out but he made me walk round the kitchen with the green top hanging down. He laughed at me in contempt, humiliating me.

After that he let me rest a while, and get dressed to go out. I have a good figure and like to show it off in tight leather or deerskin trousers with no panties, or else short narrow skirts in the same material. For the top I have a bolero that laces up the front, showing my bosom to advantage. He is proud of his 'sexy wife' as he calls me in front of strangers, and we walked through the village to a rather expensive restaurant, an old coaching house.

I liked this part of it, because after the meal he ordered me onto the stage where I did a striptease; it was really a sort of belly dance during which I removed the clothes very slowly until I was naked. Then he told me to lie on a table which has been prepared meanwhile. Whereupon any men who wish to, were free to use me for their pleasure. As usual I was frantic and came off several times as they fucked and sucked me everywhere, until my husband called a halt.

That, in a manner of speaking, is how I would like it to happen! Now I would like to explain my sex life as it really is.

I live with a chap, but we are not married and are free to sleep around if we like. Actually it doesn't occur often, because he loves me and I worship him. It's as simple as that. I have to confess I am mad keen on sex, and can't get enough of it. Which suits him because he's always got his prick in the air, in a manner of speaking. I took to him at once, as my nose can sniff out virility like a Dordogne pig snuffles for truffles. And the consequence of that is that I let him do whatever he wants with me. I'm the complete sex object, and that's the way we both prefer it. I'm his popsy, he's my pop-up!

He is pretty kinky, in the sense that he likes it on the move, usually in the living room. I wait for him like Madame Recamier, but he pulls me off and makes me bend over, my bottom high in the air. He paws me all over, especially my breasts which he knows brings me on, then when I'm ready he inserts his penis in my vagina. Joined together, we walk slowly round, him upright and me like a sort of spider. It's tiring for me but his thing inside me makes me so excited I keep going as long as I can. I have generous breasts and he gets a thrill playing with them when we halt; thanks to him my nipples are as big as the tip of my little finger now. Of course, by about the third stop I'm so randy I have an orgasm. But he holds back! We move into the bedroom and I lay my arms on the dressing table, him still inside me. I have to look at myself in the mirror, which I didn't like to do at first but he made me. He likes me to fondle my hair and apply my make-up, especially lipstick, and seems to get a special delight in all the shiny women's things on the dresser. Then usually he withdraws and takes some of my juices up to my anus, making it yield with his fingers until he reckons he can put his piece of meat in. By this time it is huge and, without fail, every time he hurts me when he enters; but he does it so slowly that I can feel him all the way, and the

83

dull pain brings on another orgasm. I would miss this now if he stopped the practice. He likes me to remain completely passive, while he pokes me in both orifices as the mood takes him, until I'm gasping and saying 'yes, yes' and 'no, stop', and I don't know whether I'm coming or going. Sometimes I'm so exhausted I sink to my knees, but he hauls me up again, dragging me to a chair which he sits on with me still attached. Now it's my turn to bump up and down on his phallus, twisting sideways left and right, lifting up my hair and pleading with him to take his pleasure at last. Which he does with me straddling him and just about collapsing with the ultimate muscular effort I have to make. He then throws me off and I seek the cool smoothness of the floor tiles, pressing my body full-length upon them, while he prepares the bed where we recover on our backs, side by side, hand in hand. I sometimes think he gets his greatest pleasure from seeing me spread out and panting on the floor at the end. He loves to see me cringe.

There is no doubt he could be a dangerous man if he didn't have me to hurt. You have probably guessed that he thrashes me, and I love it. We have our own signals so that we vary it: on the bottom, across my breasts, between my legs. It's quite an art and also involves him trailing the leather whip across various parts, or tying it tight around my middle or my thigh; even using it like a saw along my crack. Once he put a stick in my anus, another time an ice-cube in my vagina. He is a genuine sadist.

But there are tender moments too. For example when I spend ages fondling and sucking and licking his prick, so that he sometimes ejaculates into my mouth. Or when he kneels on all fours with his genitals over my mouth, and I play with his scraggy bag thing, while he amuses himself biting and licking my sex.

If you love each other, anything goes, that's what I say. I have had the good fortune to meet a man who has as much appetite as I have, whose life is governed by the orgasm and everything linked to it. Even when I was a teen-age girl I liked physical movement most of all, and today I am crazy about dancing; incidentally I learned to do the splits properly, and I adore the moment when my vulva touch the blessed coolness of the floor tiles. I create new dance steps all the time, making sure they are graceful, I give my performances to huge imaginary audiences, or to an audience of just one – my man!

Nevertheless, the peak of achievement is the successful orgasm, when reality and dreams coincide. It has to be both together, or you are just animals. This calls for a sustained effort and brain power.

So many people fail to take sex seriously, but we think life is sex and vice-versa. And when two people are truly fond of each other, it's Long Live Love!

Jacky Dance

On The Cote D'Azur

The sense of freedom is making me sing like a bird. I have left my husband and stepped out of my clothes!

Wherever true Paradise may be, I have come close to it on the Mediterranean shore. The sun is at its zenith on this marvellous summer day painted by Van Gogh and smelling like the Garden of Eden. Those pines! I am admiring, too, the human body; in fact dozens of them naked and brown as berries at this nudist camp that has liberated Man and Woman.

We are free in our relaxed movements, free in our communing with nature, free in our affinity with one another because we are healthy and not ashamed.

But let me explain. I left my husband two months ago because I could stand it no longer. I had grown to hate this old-style phallocrat. You know the type: sliding his hand up waitresses' skirts and pinching maids' bottoms, while expecting his faithful spouse to spend her days and nights waiting on him. That's what wives are for, and woe to them if their eyes stray to the business partner while they are serving the soup.

Well, I've broken out of prison, and gone crazy in the process. Crazy? We shall see when the Great Reckoning comes! I had to put as many kilometres as I could between myself and the phallocrat, and it was French Railways who did it for me. Trains have always excited me, you get to meet such extraordinary people. Which is how I came to be chatting with a couple of young English boys and the girl with them.

They were honest-looking and so completely carefree. For some reason hard to understand, they took to me at once, and I was in no mood to philosophize about it. The outcome was that instead of thinking things over rather grimly in some stuck-up hotel in Cannes, I agreed to join them at this *camp naturiste*. I think it was one of the most important moments in my entire existence when I made that decision.

When we arrived I invested in a tent for the duration, however long that might be, and we besported ourselves together. When I say together, I mean specifically with William, a cheerful lad with long sandy tresses and beard and a flat stomach that would make any woman narrow her eyes and melt. We swam together, ran along the beach with out hair streaming out behind us, lazed for hours getting our tan all over. Then in the evenings we wandered along the beach, had a whisky or two at a primitive bar, and then paired off.

I had always been straight-laced, whatever my fantasies, and I had a moment's hesitation when William accompanied me to my tent. But when you are both as God made you, it is impossible to take a firm stand on etiquette. Before I realized quite what was happening, I found myself in my sleeping bag with him, my hands and arms trembling to his light touch. He had soft long-fingered hands, the sort I had always secretly wanted running over me. I breathed in his fresh salt aroma and made no resistance when he lifted my chin to kiss me. I had not been kissed like that for years, and within seconds I was not only responding but exchanging tongue kisses. Our age gap disappeared and we were simply a boy and girl hungry for each others' bodies. It was something quite new to me, having a tongue lick me all over my face, neck and arms. I gave myself up to it and decided I wanted to taste him as well, sucking the salt from his chest and tight firm abdomen.

William would have seduced a whole convent of nuns, but I must confess that when his tongue actually touched my sex, I gave a jump. A conscience formed from the age of seven onwards made me hold myself back; I had learned that outside marriage there are limits. Petting yes, heavy petting no. And after I was married, the flirting was verbal only. I realize now that William knew all about my misgivings, and forced my legs open just sufficiently at exactly the moment when I could have spoiled everything. A few words of flattery and encouragement, and I surrendered myself to his attentions. It was exquisite and I drifted off on cloud of pleasure, hardly noticing that he shifted round so that his organ was close to my own mouth. A friend of mine had told me that prostitutes would take men's penises into their mouths; I had never done it in my life, but the heady aroma an inch or two from my nostrils was irresistible. We were lying on our side and William had his head between my thighs. I summoned up my courage and pursed my lips, shifting my head slightly until they enveloped the end of his member. The skin protecting it slid back and I had it in my mouth. Embarrassed in spite of myself I let it slip out again but immediately thought that was unfair and began to lick it, actually holding the stem between my fingers. With mounting excitement I sucked in more and more. It seemed very thick and was giving little jerks. The knowledge that I had the power to give this lovely boy pleasure brought an incredible pleasure for me, and I realized I was having a long sweet orgasm of a kind I had never experienced so far. And we'd hardly done anything yet!

Suddenly William moved and I feared I had done something wrong, but he was poised over me, pushing my legs far apart, and I knew he was going to enter me. I couldn't keep still and my heart was thumping, while he was panting hard. From then on I relied on him and was already imagining him inside me. He penetrated me with little thrusts and I was possessed of the Devil, forcing myself up and making him go right in. I grabbed the flesh round his waist, and then dug my nails into his bottom, forgetting everything but his hard persistent prick. I can't say whether I cried out, and in any case I was beyond caring. I can't even say what he did, except that he withdrew and changed position to penetrate me much deeper. He surrounded me with his flesh, our mouths hurting and hurting as they writhed in unison. He massaged my breasts and they hurt too, causing me to bump my pubis against him until I felt him swell and gasp, spending himself within me.

We grew calm, nibbling each other affectionately. I drifted off into a paradise of my own, caressing his hair and losing all sense of time. Eventually he helped me up and we ran to the water, where we jumped and danced about like two children bursting with joy.

We ran back to Diana and Michael in their tent, where my companions started mumbling away in an English that was lost on me. Michael poured out some mint tea in glasses, and we drank it, the two youths each with his girl against him. William pushed me towards his friend and said: 'He does it well too, he wants you.' This I understood! I smiled at Michael with parted lips, and it was a matter of a split second before he was pinching my nipples and laying me down on his sleeping bag. His mouth enveloped a breast and I was astonished to find another mouth at the other. I closed my eyes and fondled the second head of hair – Diana's! I had always imagined I would be shocked at sexual relations with another woman, but she was gentler than Michael and I found it delicious. By now, William was biting my clitoris and sucking hard on it. Waves of pleasure went up and down my torso. I was gasping out words incoherently: 'Oui, more, please, please do it. Oh c'est super!' Michael took William's place and penetrated me in a single hung thrust, groaning and chewing at my shoulder. He seemed to be ripping me apart and I passed out, recovering to find Michael smiling down at me: 'Is that good?' I simply gaped at him. 'Are you alright?' I could only sigh feebly. Diana and William were growling like wild beasts as they came. A sharp smell of semen enveloped us. We all stumbled down to the water and this restored ut.

I knew, of course, that women can have several orgasms in a row. I was shivering when we got back to the tent, and Diana rubbed me dry with a large towel. We looked into each other's eyes and knew we wanted to do it together. Diana had superb blue-green eyes, jet black eyebrows and long lashes. Her raven hair was in loose curls and she had thick succulent lips. How I wanted to kiss those lips! At school a girl once tried to kiss me and I pushed her away, utterly disgusted at the idea. Now I wanted Diana, she was so beautiful; I was still itching from her mouth on my breast. Not only that, her bosom was big and firm, her nipples erect from the seawater and, on an impulse I went to her, rubbing my own aching breasts against her silky tits. She laughed happily, took my head in her hands and planted a cool fruity kiss on my mouth. It was divine. We sat down and she looked at me, trying to decide what to do. As soft as seaweed, her fingers began fluttering all over me, while she kissed me several times and said: 'You're lovely,' and I said she was beautiful. Diana quickened my blood as no-one previous, and I felt I was being eaten alive. She was so expert, she knew exactly when I wanted her to knead my breasts and arms, and that I wanted her to go on and on. It must have been at least five minutes before she relented.

Laying me down at last and covering me with her body, she squashed my breasts with hers and rocked up and down. She kissed me passionately, taking the lead although I was her senior. 'You're so innocent,' she said, and I noticed she opened her legs, placing them either side of my body. I was stroking her voluptuous pussy, but dare I venture lower and do what I longed to do – explore the crack beneath the thick hair now poised over my middle? Would she be offended, was she only playing at sex, mocking me? Hesitantly, I touched the dark frizzy hair and found the cleft. Her lips were fat and juicy, like her mouth, and she was warm and flaccid. As Diana showed no resistance, I did to her what I had so often done to myself, rubbing her where I knew she would like it. I pushed my fingers farther in, wetting them with her juice, and she came with a long drawn out sigh. She pushed my hand away and nimbly sat on a nearby cushion spreading her legs indecently. I needed no further bidding and greedily licked and sucked at her splayed opening, nuzzling with my nose. This was not enough for me, and I simultaneously massaged her heavy bosom. Diana continued howling like a cat on heat, and suddenly a male hand was gliding under my exposed bottom into my own cleft, followed by a thick prick.

Things happened fast then. Michael flung me to one side and fell upon Diana, as William seized my waist with one arm and rubbed my clitoris hard. I exploded instantly. Subsequent events are still unclear in my mind. The four of us became a mass of bodies, we were a single act of love, a single raging phallo-uterus that was sharing, giving, receiving pleasure such as I had never imagined. Sometime later we had a quick bathe and collapsed into sleep. I was the first to wake, the dawn well past. I lay there aware of every inch of my sore body. I was happy, beautiful, loving, innocent and triumphant. I laughed, waking William.

'Wassermarrer?' I had to guess what that meant!

'Nossing,' I gurgled. 'I fill so 'appy.' He got the message. Even at that stage, I would never have told him that this wonderful night might never have been, had they told me in the train that they wanted me for a sex party. I would have been too shocked to consent.

William dozed off and I gazed fondly down on him. Then I stole out and walked and trotted along the beach alone, the waves of the Mediterranean lapping the shore half-heartedly. The water was chilly as yet, and I splashed about, forcing myself to be brave and swim around. Michael and Diana joined me and we kissed good morning, then struck out from the shore. We came out clean as new pins, to find William starting breakfast. I went right to him, kissed him fondly and said I loved him even more than I did yesterday. He said: 'I love you too, Stephanie.'

This idyllic new life was interrupted shortly after writing the foregoing account. A letter arrived to remind me of my 'responsibilities'. My lawyer wanted proof of my husband's 'misconduct'. In a way I disliked providing the evidence, as it was unfair on Benoit, in view of what I'd been up to! But the man had been so selfish, so indifferent to my needs, that I went ahead, took the train back to Paris to produce the necessary witnesses.

Three days later my mission accomplished. I phoned the *camp*, confirmed that my English friends were still there, and left a message asking them to wait for me ...

Stephanie

Country Foursome

As it eventually reached me, the story was totally plausible. I was fairly close to Helene, and I knew that she was capable of pulling out all the stops to get her man, once she had decided she wanted him.

She may not have been the world's most beautiful woman, but she made up for it in sex-appeal, especially on that torrid July evening as the four made their way out to Maxence's country place 40 kilometres from Marseilles.

Let me make it clear that Maxence's wife is Claire and they are both doctors. Helene is married to Julien, who is something to do with property.

Helene had managed to get herself the passenger seat next to Maxence, and this may well have put ideas into all four minds later on.

It all started off innocently enough, except possibly on the part of Helene whose white cotton shift was so thin you could clearly make out her coffee-coloured nipples beneath the material. You might almost think she wore no panties, but close inspection would have revealed a little triangle of cloth between her legs, held in position by a string arrangement round her waist and in the crack of her bottom.

Doctors have a certain charisma, of course, but Maxence also had a powerful masculine odour about him which was driving her mad with desire that evening.

Talking of driving, Maxence was flinging the car round bend after bend. The woman at his side had omitted to fasten her safety belt, with the result that her left thigh gently pressed into Maxence's right thigh whichever way the road twisted. So much so that she had to spread her legs to keep in position – and for another reason she was only too aware of!

It was still hot, though the worst of the day was over. The sun's rays made entrancing shadows over the Provence landscape, where about five billion grasshopers were kicking up one hell of a din, probably because there wasn't much grass to hop around in. Everyone was parched and longing for that cooling drink 30 minutes hence.

For some time, Helene had been watching Maxence's reactions out of the corner of her eye, wondering if he was actually aware of their leg contact.

Suddenly he said: 'Not afraid of a fast driver, I hope. You're not saying much.'

'I prefer fast drivers,' she said. 'Adore them.'

The double-meaning was lost on Maxence, too busy with the wheel and the column-mounted gearchange. He was riding the vehicle like a horse whose every quirk he knew. Helene relapsed into silence, resolved not to force the pace. She massaged the back of her legs, where the muscles seemed to be pulling from her ankles to her crotch.

Her discomfort prevented her looking round at Claire and her husband who was humming a catchy tune. From time to time he broke off to bestow a light kiss on his companion's sunburned arm, just where it was perspiring at the elbow. Claire smiled at him, acquiescing to his boyish whim, but it was enough to start her off on a train of thought.

They flashed through Bandol, the ochre and white houses resembling curios on the shelves of a giftshop. And then Maxence was pulling up inside the main gates, he jumped out and closed them, finally easing the car along the drive to avoid kicking up a dust.

Night fell within minutes, and Maxence switched on the garden lamps. The two men brought out the table onto the tiled *terrasse*, and the women went over to the fountain. A miniature dolphin soared into the air as Helene plunged her arms in the water, evoking cries of delight from both women. They went back to the *terrasse* and kicked off their sandals. A lizard eyed them from a crack in the wall of the old house.

Helene remembered a passage from a poem by the Comtesse de Noailles: 'Blue lizards ran over the antique pillars with a precision so warm, so gay, so diligent, that the imposing destiny of the lethargic stones seemed to take on new life from the silver veins ...'

Maxence burst in on her meditation: 'What's on your mind?'

'Poetry – eternal things ...'

'Well, don't let it worry you too much, first things first. How about laying the table!'

Helene and Claire did as they were told. They opened the thick wooden shutters and went into the cool interior of what was once a farmhouse. The spouses piled plates, glasses and cutlery on a trolley and wheeled it onto the *terrasse*.

'Let's dance for a while first,' Helene suggested.

'Good idea.'

They girated outside where the speakers were installed, Maxence with Helene, Julien with Claire. As the music undulated across the Provence pinewoods, so the couples writhed like snakes, their pelvises glued together in scarce-concealed masturbatory intent. Helene shifted her position, her breasts coming to rest higher on Maxence's ribcage, a gesture her partner countered by slipping her shoulder straps down her upper arm. Helene replaced them with a demure lowering of her eyes, thinking that it never did any harm to keep a man guessing, and that the longer the decorum lasted the better the descent into debauchery – if such was to be the subsequent turn of events. To underline her point she left her partner to prepare some iced drinks for them all, Kirs consisting of white wine and blackcurrant juice. Having done this, she came back with the tray of drinks, forcing everyone to break off.

With every appearence of naivety she said: 'Aren't we going to dance some more?'

'Not hungry yet?' asked her husband.

'It's still hot.'

They resumed the dance and the Kir had its effect, providing just that extra courage they all needed. Maxence again slipped down Helene's shoulder straps, she raised her arms and the flimsy dress crumpled to the tiles, revealing everything except the triangle of cloth. Maxence tugged at the string and this too fell away.

'You shouldn't have done that,' said Helene, 'Julien

94

may not like it.'

Julien however was at that instant undoing Claire's dress buttons, the cue for Maxence to paw Julien's wife to his heart's content. The wife-swap was under way, the two spouses naked, the men still clothed. Helene had always regarded the fulfillment of her lust as a primary pleasure in life, and from the moment she consented she had rejected all notions of sin, danger and conscience . The only real crime in her view was the inability to say yes when you wanted sex with a man you desired. With the green light shining brightly, she gave generous and total consent to Maxence's caresses. He led her to a large pinetree near the *terrasse* and placed her against it, pushing her legs apart. With an alacrity that surprised her, he was out of his clothes in 10 seconds flat and down on his knees administering to his latest patient, extracting her bud of passion with his knife-like tongue. 'You're soaking already,' he diagnosed. 'Are you coming?'

'Don't talk, go on, for God's sake don't stop, I've been soaking since we left Marseilles!'

The music had come to an end, and the air was full of the insect's endless complaint.

Helene whimpered in dismay: 'Oh please Max, I can't wait, I'll faint if I don't come soon.' She seized his head and forced it harder against herself, then pulled them both down on the bed of pine needles. 'Oh don't torture me!' In her frustration she seized Max's own needle, rubbing it furiously and emitting short cries, on the verge of weeping. Then in a surge of primitive desire, Max threw her legs back and out, thrusting his weapon into her without further preliminaries. She came at once, and then wordlessly got onto her knees, presenting her buttocks to him. More carefully, he sodomized her, himself taking his pleasure.

Afterwards she clung to him as they knelt together: 'Oh Max, if you only knew how I like that. Julien does it but it's become routine, it's never like it was then.'

They lay there on the needles, enjoying their soreness. They both said, 'I'm hungry,' at the same moment, and burst out laughing. They were still kissing ardently when the others shouted from the house.

'That's enough of that, dinner is served! It's what we came for!'

Max and Helene ran hand in hand, Helene shouting: 'You may be right, but my word what an aperitif!'

Genevieve

Villa Eros

When your husband's away on an installation job for three weeks in Dunkerque and you live in Marseilles, nobody can expect you to live like a nun. Especially when you're just over 40, which as everyone knows is the age when a woman's appetite is positively gargantuan. Well, mine is!

I had been left on my own too many times, and resolved to do something about it. As elsewhere, Marseilles has several very particular magazines that take ads. I put one in reading: 'Lady, 40, attractive, well endowed, wishes to meet Gentlemen 40-45 skilled in erotic pleasures. No vulgar machos or adventures. Write box No ----.'

I expected a mass of replies, and I got them. After careful consideration I wrote off to a man whose elegant style and handwriting seemed to denote a broad mind and a deep understanding of women's needs and aspirations. You have to be so wary these days and I obliged him to contact me by phone only, so that we could give an outline of our appearance and intentions. So it was that our first meeting proved an immense success, and we drank to our future with a bottle of pink champagne.

His name was Jean and, having read the book *Emmanuelle* half a dozen times, he declared that he would be my 'mentor'. During a second meeting he told me he had fixed up for us to go to a place called the Villa Eros near Cannes, where they ran 'bacchanalia' as he elegantly termed them.

I was game for anything, on the grounds that you only live once, and I threw caution to the winds when we slipped through the front door on that spring evening in 1981. The centrepiece inside was a good quality dance floor, where perhaps a dozen couples were creeping round to the soft swingy American music. It was out of a Hollywood film, with quiet lighting for discretion, and to help the shy ones. We weren't keen to drink too much, and went straight onto the dance floor when the music changed to a tango. Everyone was close-hauled as you might say, with couples occasionally kissing and one or two actually groping each other. We broke off for a drink at the bar, where they were serving *sangria*, which as we all know is a noted aphrodisiac. Every now and again, there was a soft loudspeaker announcement saying there was room for two or perhaps three more couples upstairs.

After a while, Jean suggested we go up, and I said OK if he felt like it, and he said his expectations were rising fast. Always put things politely, he did, being a man of education. I had rather a shock when we got there, the floor was covered with mattresses. There was hardly any light, and this was deliberate of course. We undressed and occupied a mattress that was still warm, in a manner of speaking. Several hands stroked and patted me as we went towards our mattress. For a while we just stayed doing nothing, listening to the heavy breathing and squeaks of delight from all around us. Then Jean lay back with his cock standing vertical. Naturally I knelt down to take it in my mouth and had only been going a few seconds when a hand clutched at my twat from behind, a part of my anatomy, I may add, that had been ready and willing since we first set foot in the establishment – I've always been sensitive to atmosphere. Well, this hand was quickly replaced by a more demanding member of ample proportions and as stiff as a rope end on the quayside in old Marseilles. The owner's pumping increased my fellating powers, to coin a phrase, and I was blessed with a couple of orgasms in quick succession.

Jean meanwhile was on the brink of ejaculating, and rolled over to pay tribute to the woman on the next mattress. However, hardly deprived of his organ, my mouth was immediately replenished with a truly splendid example of what Man is capable of. Resolved to do justice to this noble appendix, I bore down upon it, to be instantly mounted by a second stallion. I was beside myself with joy, attaining a climax quite out of this world, hitherto unknown thanks to the unaccustomed nature of the circumstances. Within the first few minutes I was sired four times, a fact that Jean later refused to believe, although he had been in Marseilles all his life. One man told me I had the fleshiest hind quarters he had seen for years, which I thought was rather a nice to thing to say. Well, we women were asking for it. As you might say, otherwise we would not have come to the Villa Eros, but I confess I was astonished at the speed the men leaped from woman to woman, mind you, we only had an hour to get it all in! Feeling the need for a change, I lay down and waited for a minute or so. A big man who was 60 if he'd seen a day appeared before my eyes, his long chopper mauve-grey from constant use, and pushed back my legs like he was trussing a chicken. In this inelegant position he endeavoured to enter me, but I had no time to worry about him, for another male knelt at my side, closing my fingers around his tool, which I wanked for him as best I could, whereupon he shoved the old Johnny out of the way and ordered me to suck him off. Alas, the hour was over too quickly, and Jean and I clumped downstairs high and dry, so to speak.

On our way back to Marseilles, Jean congratulated me on the way I had taken so naturally to the festivities. I did a far better job than his previous lady friends, he informed me. I said I was glad, and would like to join in another orgy whenever he liked, and he told me to call them 'bacchanalia'.

Now, what conclusions can I draw from the evening? To be frank, in one hour I experienced more sexual convulsions than most women enjoy in a lifetime. Prodded and belaboured in every imaginable position, I satisfied the equivalent of two rugby teams in 60 minutes flat, I reckon! I knew roughly what to expect, because Jean had explained, but I came away with the impression that we had been playing the Ride of the Walkyries at four times the normal speed. I would have liked it a little slower, but the clocks stand still only once a year, and that's in the autumn and not the spring!

My escort dropped me at my place at 1 am. I fell into a dreamy slumber, and today feel quite refreshed, ready to collect my husband at the station.

I have no doubt he finds his own pleasure on his

frequent trips away, and I would not deprive him of it. And of course, if he doesn't, well he only has himself to blame!

Aline

Bloody Sunday

By now, everyone knows about Sunday. From the film, and the song banned from French radio because of the suicides. This particular Sunday I'm telling about was as bad as you can imagine – pouring with rain all morning. I had to traipse down all seven storeys to make sure of the general picture, as Elise and I only had one window about the size of a handkerchief. Elise is my room-mate and we're both AC-DC.

I wasn't feeling hungry and just had a piece of bread when we got up around 12. Then I went out, as I say, to call Alice from the phone-box as I'd promised after breakfast. There was hardly anyone about, only Germans and Japanese half asleep in their coaches.

I got into one of the phone-boxes and started nattering. There was a bloke in the other one and he was nattering too. But he smiled a bit and blew me a kiss. He looked effeminate, pretty more like, harmless anyway. So I put my tongue out, just for politeness. Crafty sod, he came out the same time as I did and he said a girl he knew had gone in for mental treatment. I commiserated and bucked him up a bit, feeling quite confident really after the pep pills I had taken.

To cut a long story short we went to the flicks to see *La Maman Et La Putain*. There weren't many in the audience and we were on our own, so it wasn't surprising he started touching me up in front. I pushed his hand away a couple of times which was the normal thing, and then took pity on him and let him go ahead. Of course I enjoyed it too, as he was delicate about it, but I wouldn't let him go any further. At least, that's what I intended, but he worked me up so much that when he slid his hand under my skirt I hardly did anything to stop him. After all there was no harm in it. He went 'Mmm' when he found I wore stockings – I never wear tights because Elise doesn't like that. Anyway he fingered me without stopping for the last half hour, and I had to hitch my skirt up at the back so as

101

not to stain it.

I agreed to go back to his place, and in the lift I saw for the first time that he wore make-up. No wonder he smelled nice! He pushed against me and said he wanted to have a tumble with me. But imagine my surprise when I discovered another bloke in his flat, and I assumed he was his boyfriend. The place was white with black furniture and red curtains. I shivered, maybe because it felt damp owing to all the plants they had.

Oh, by the way, his name was Christian and his mate was Bernard. We drank whisky and stuff and they told me to get on the bed. I did this and they petted me all over and fingered my clothes like I was a doll. Bernard who wore nail varnish talked to me softly and kissed my face while Christian removed my clothing item by item very slowly, working me up so much I wanted to giggle. Then Christian drew away and let Bernard lick me between the legs, muttering things abut my sexy stockings. I felt really dizzy and let them put me on my knees with Bernard still chewing away at my clit, then turning round under me and bringing me down on his prick. We both came, and then Christian sodomized me so gently I hardly knew it was happening.

They must have put something in the last drink because I began to feel sick and said I wanted to leave. They said there was no question of it, and I started to struggle, getting scared. I remember Bernard fucked me again with Christian holding me down. I yelled and he clamped a hand over my mouth. Bernard let go inside me and Christian said it was a shame I didn't come and masturbated me. I knew about homos, of course, how they were decent unless you upset them, so I just lay there and let Christian keep rubbing me, saying 'No, no' all the time. He told me I could go now if I liked, but just then I began tossing about and came.

They poured out more drinks and soon lolled hopelessly on the bed. They tied my wrists to the bedstead with neckties, and they kept kissing and licking me between the legs for what seemed hours. I was in a sort of coma and let Bernard poke me again, with Christian sodomizing

Bernard. I can't recall it very clearly, but I believe we all had our orgasms together, finishing upon the floor laughing dead drunk.

We slept it off and then they took me into the bathroom, with just a little water in the bath. I started blubbing but Christian ordered me to suck him off and put my fingers in his bottom. After which they left me lying in the bath and ejaculated over me, both of them. The place was stinking of spunk and drink and tobacco and I said I had to leave and get ready for a lecture. They said would I do them a favour and watch them. Which I did while they made love to each other, stroking their backs for them.

I crept up to our flat about eight o'clock that Monday morning, after a large coffee inside the cafe opposite. The cat meowed a bit even though Elise had fed him. She left a note telling me not to be a *pute* and stay out all night. I was late for the first lecture and felt like death warmed up all day.

That evening we went to bed early, and I said I felt miserable, so we cuddled up together. She's a lovely girl with a wonderful disposition and smells of lemon. During the night she started feeling me as I didn't want it I pretended to be in a deep sleep.

Next morning I felt fine and we had breakfast with toast and fig jam, which I adore. It was Tuesday and I had to attend more lectures, but I couldn't concentrate, thinking of Sunday night.

Lily

THE LINGUISTICS
OF LOVE

The Building Site

We had plenty of time ahead of us that Saturday night, when I agreed to nip onto the piece of waste land with you. They were putting up a block of flats and we chose a wall that was not too dirty.

You were in your blue suit and I in my brick-red jersey dress! To start with I let you take the initiative, which meant leaning back against the wall imprisoned between your arms either side of my head; the classic pose, with the boy using kisses as a pretext for rubbing himself against the girl.

Standing, tense at first, cloth against cloth, we made little movements and chatted idly about the dance. But I could feel your hard bulge pushing and pushing against my mound, as I arched my back, my legs slightly apart and straining against the wall. Loving to be wooed, I made it difficult for you to insert your hand, and clasp one breast then the other. To tell you it was OK with me, I dug my nails into your neck and exchanged spittle with you. But you knew I might alter my mind and with infinite caution you took out one hand and let it glide down to my abdomen, but no farther for the moment. You preferred to concentrate on my nipples, knowing they are the quickest way to a girls's sex. I made tiny movements with my hands on your back, using my palms. You seemed unsure and I swiftly found your zip, running it down and feeling your thing inside. I sensed the beginnings of desire at that moment, realizing so completely the pressure of the male. My randiness increased with the sensation of doing wrong.

You uncovered my breasts and the night air made me shiver just a little. I quivered as you slowly pulled by briefs down over my hips, your gesture concealed under the soft folds of my dress skirt.

I wanted you to do it at once, but I would never have dreamed of asking you. Instead I moved my middle away to make you work harder. I wanted to come, but not too

107

soon. I wanted to savour my power, enjoy the influence I had over you. I was God and the Devil at the same time, capable of playing hot or cold, perfidious as a snake, able to spoil everything and humiliate you who are so proud of your vigour. I wanted you to suffer while the alchemy of love-making ran its course. It was I who would conquer you, make you my slave to humiliate, even as my longing came in waves from a secret place you dared not reach yet. Oh yes, you could have left me standing, but you lusted for me too much to snatch your body away. You sensed my underlying contempt as I allowed myself to be courted.

Still you hesitated, your chest thumping, your stomach in anguish, fearing to make a mess of it. To keep you on the boil I lifted my thigh, stepped out of my briefs, and you nervously undid your belt letting your trousers fall. My thigh forced you apart and I lifted your testicles, then jostled them two or three times, so that you gasped in fear of premature ejaculation. In a gesture close to panic you fumbled under my skirt and found my crack with a finger, then two, pushing them into the dripping grotto. It felt so sweet for me, and I kept my thigh against your crotch, swinging it gently from side to side. I wouldn't let you pull down your underpants, and this drove you frantic.

I offered my lips again and you responded feverishly, inserting your tongue, which I greedily sucked into my mouth. Then, as if it was your idea, you licked my neck, flicked at my nipples, one-two, opening your mouth wide and biting gently. You would have liked to bite harder, like a hungry wolf, but you knew you mustn't overdo it because I might yet reject you for being clumsy.

Then you became impatient, undoing the front of my dress, licking my navel, nibbling between my thighs and finally plunging your face into the fiery breath of my sex. I wanted to cry out, but I controlled the urge, enjoying your skill in wiggling your tongue where you know a girl likes it best. I am starting to lose the details, but I know you made your tongue go stiff to penetrate farther. Your whole face seemed to have buried itself in my bush. Your hands kneaded my bottom and, as a shock wave hit me, I pushed forward. Your breath was steamy and you gulped noisily as I spread my legs wide in abandon, as you pulled at my bottom, opening the crack. Alas you withdrew and I clutched at your black hair, wishing your whole head would penentrate me. Mercifully you resumed licking the length of my vulva, furiously, so that I could not stop myself squeaking. It seemed my entrails were scorching, thirsty for cool water.

In the distance a bus drew up, and there were voices. Oh no, don't stop now, they won't come here! Yes, yes, faster, wetter, cool me, cool me! I can't stand it – fuck me!!!

Only then did I reveal my yearning, disclose my dependence on you. Oh do it now, please, I told you, clinging to your neck and placing my thighs outside yours. You must, you must, do it now! I remember I was so impatient I jiggled until I felt your firm stem penetrate me, and then bumped against you, not caring if I broke your backbone. Your penis jumped out because I wanted to play some more, and I drew back. I made yelping noises and twisted my torso so that my breasts hurt against your ribs. If only this could go on all night, I thought, as I drowned in the ocean of your passionate embrace.

You had not come yet, had not really penetrated me. I was dying for it. I could have smoked a cigar with my cunt! I became a power-crazed harpie, a tart, a slut, a she-cat on heat. Using you for my pleasure, I kissed you under the arms, breathed in your virile smell, bit your sweaty tits. I stopped and gulped at your fierce frustrated prick, pulling at it with my lips, as if it was my last chance ever to do it to a man. You began moaning and jerking, and I found my fingers imprisoned in your rear crack, held tight by your straining muscles clutching and clenching.

Then I let you have me! Oh, the supreme moment when you roared like a beast in pain and your pelvis pistonned back and forth as I sucked your male cream through my vagina into the furnace of my womb.

We collapsed together with a cry, death in our eyes, the Deity revolving in the black night. And then we looked at the stars.

Maren Sell

Having Lunch Together

Across the lunch table she had no idea I was forcing her lips open with my mouth, imagining myself raping her lips, seeking her tongue.

'Give me your tongue, oh please give it me!' I heard myself saying. Actually, she merely took another sip at her wine.

You are shy but I can almost feel you sliding your tongue forward. It is sweet and soft and swims like a fish in my mouth. I want to swallow it. Now I have you at my mercy, and I order you to take off your shirt. You say nothing, but your eyes are mesmerized, cannot leave my own. 'Take off your petticoat,' I scold. I'm teasing, because you can't take it off, for your hands are lashed together behind your back. I insist: 'That's why I've got you here, take it off!'

You can only stretch, arching your back and offering me your breasts under the thin material. You wait, scarcely able to breathe with terror. Now I tear the garment off you, and I see your bosom quiver like two jellies. Your face goes white when I run my hands over your skin. I pinch your nipples and they harden, I flick them, suck on them in turn, bite them so that it hurts you and you bite your top lip. You cannot resist me, you stuck-up bitch. You are so weak and helpless and I yearn to hit you, to make you cry out in pain so that I can make love to you all the more passionately afterwards. Don't you know about sadists? I strike you several times, and you are no longer passive; you look at me wide-eyed, dumb and terrified. I bite your breasts fiercely, taking in whole mouthfuls, and you struggle to get free and you can't. The bonds are hurting your wrists, and you move forward, attempting to push me away, and I bite your breasts even harder. It is extremely painful for you, you are shaking. Then you go limp again and I stop. After that I step back and sit on a chair facing you, looking at you intently. You feel faint and lean back against the wall, trying to think of a way out. The soreness in your breasts has descended lower, and luxuriously you part your legs, throw your head back, so that your body is straining towards me, your quim inches from my mouth. You want me to hurt you again, but I have forbidden you to speak. I can hear you breathing deeply, and you are hot all over. That's how I want you – fluid.

'And what would you like for dessert, ladies?' asked the waiter. 'A chocolate charlotte, I think.' Said Marie-Joelle.
  'And you, Madam?'

I advanced my hand, sliding it down your front, fluttering around your quim. Again, I kiss you, my tongue penetrating your soft warm mouth, pillaging you. Your whole body is a ripe fruit, and I am going to pluck it. Oh my word, I can't keep my legs together!

'Strawberries please, and cream and sugar.' I said.
  The waiter left us. Two o'clock already, and it was very close, probably about to rain. I smiled at Marie-Joelle, the elegant smartly dressed bourgeoise who never did a thing wrong in her life.
  'You're so lucky being slim,' she said. 'I really must cut out these sweet things, but I do so adore chocolate.' She laughed in a refined sort of way. She had certainly had a glass too many to drink.
  'Oh, I think you should always pamper yourself as far as possible, don't you agree, darling?'
  'I'm sure you're absolutely right.' She was delighted with my reaction, she felt less guilty.

Now you are on my bed, your face in the pillow and your bottom indecently in the air, like a mare on heat. I kiss your fat round cheeks one after the other, smell you, delicately part your crevice and lick your anus, trailing my tongue from your sex upwards, time and again. You are so excited you cannot keep still, and your vulva slowly parts and grows moist – for me.
  'I am all yours, do what you like with me,' you moan.

111

My pulse quickens, lust races through my veins, and I fall upon you nuzzling you with my mouth, eyes, ears, nostrils. Your woman's smell inebriates me and I am weak and limp.

She was still guzzling her chocolate.

'Would you care for some coffee, ladies?' asked the waiter.

'Two expressos, and the bill please,' I said.

'There's a photo exhibition I'd very much like to see. Not far away, if you'd like to come with me.'

My God she hasn't caught on! All I'm thinking of is her against the wall in my flat! Oh how I want to hit her, make it hurt!

'Of course, Marie-Joelle,' I said, 'I'd love to. And then we'll go back to my place for tea.'

'I think that's a marvellous idea.'

She chuckled gaily and I joined in her excitement. We got up from the table. Outside, in the Rue Royale, it had started to rain.

Linda Dangoor

A Dream

Six o'clock, the afternoon's over. Three discreet taps on the door say so. Those taps mean I must get ready for the evening, which means my husband must have looked at me in that special way when he came home feigning indifference at lunch time.

My big problem is whether the twinkle in his eye is because of the new dress or the new hair style. What does it matter? All I need do is to wear exactly the same things as the woman who attracted him those few hours ago. I take a bath, with the lavender bathsalts as usual, and dive into the wardrobe for everything I need, including the gold shoes I haven't even worn since I tried them on in the shop.

I can imagine already how the evening will work out. As I appear in the doorway of the *salon*, I receive an admiring look from my husband and his colleagues. They wave me to a seat at a pedestal table where my preferred aperitif is waiting, along with the caviar, salmon and white cheese sandwiches. We converse enthusiastically for about an hour and then move into the dining room where I stand waiting for my husband to push the chair under me. As he approaches his velvet black eyes glisten, and he sneaks a touch of my wrist or the nape of my neck with his aristocratic hands. He will remark to his colleagues how radiant I look, how fair my skin, how sophisticated my hair, how impeccable my dress and accessories.

But of course I am no Dresden china figure, and my reputation as a joyous companion and *bonne vivante* where it comes to food and drink needs no stressing. I have a reputation to keep up: that of finding the *mot juste* for every dish as it arrives, every wine as it is offered. As we gourmets warm to our meal, the guests are unaware that my husband's hand often strays to my knees, parting them as far as I allow, and stroking the insides of my thighs – often as far as the top of my stockings! This never fails to excite me and I am most embarrassed trying to pretend that nothing irregular is happening. I can only smile back at him as I continue eating, wriggling forward a little even so, enabling him to reach higher.

After the meal we take champagne in the *salon*, which the servants have arranged. The musicians are already playing some Chopin, and two professional dancers are performing some ballet steps. We sit or recline on divans as the mood takes us, having our champagne poured for us by a steward. Small lamps around the room with lovely mid-red shades add to the intimacy of the occasion. In due course we dance, exchanging partners as we like, until such time as my dear husband gives me the signal and we steal away. Perhaps he had 'ordered' his friends not to notice!

I can never be sure what will follow. Sometimes we go for a swim together in our pool outside, or we retire to our bedroom, flinging ourselves together on the bed or on the large deep-piled carpet, depending on my husbands whim that evening. Naturally, I cannot reveal the details of our night of love. Suffice to say that we continue our dalliance throughout the following day, as often as not, and then spend a second night of pleasure. We doze and eat snacks as the spirit moves us.

On the second morning there is always a little gift waiting for me. We part and I wait for the evening at six o'clock on whichever day he again wishes to claim his conjugal rights. Between times I go about my duties, wearing only a housecoat. If I want to, I read a novel or do a crossword puzzle in my boudoir, slipping on a simple dress for a light meal from time to time ...

It's a marvellous dream, but I come to my senses at last, realizing that the three taps on my door were those of my son, whose job it is to wake me.

The grim reality is that I have to go down and get breakfast for the children, and do my husband's sandwiches for him to take to work. Then there's the cat's tray to clean, and his food to put out, as well as the dog's. I shall be busy making beds and washing up and cleaning and doing a hundred other jobs. Which will take me to 5.30 when I do running repairs and wait for my husband to

114

arrive half an hour later.

And yet, on some days I go for a stroll in the park, or if it's raining I join some friends for a game of cards or Scrabble or chess which I'm quite good at.

As I wait for my husband to come in I can hear the TV sets going on, and the clink of dishes and crockery as people prepare for the evening.

Unless my husband's in the mood for love, I spend the evening reading or carrying on with the novel I am writing but may never finish.

But every day I spend an hour at the hairdresser's or at the beauty parlour, meaning to stay young and attractive as long as I can.

Gisele Tchilinguirian

My First Trip To Vienna

I had never left my country, Morocco, hardly been outside Casablanca, never known any man but my husband to sleep with, and I tried not to think about growing old.

Then one day this wonderful thing happened to me.

We had to make a trip to Vienna to see a friend of my husband's in a hurry. I had looked forward to it so much during the flight, my first trip in a plane, but the people we met were so dull and by the third day I was consumed with boredom. Having to be on my best behaviour all the time made it worse.

We had a car and chauffeur at our disposal and on the afternoon in question I had this mad idea of going to some swish coffee house and stuffing myself with as many cakes as I could swallow. I begged the keys from the chauffeur and stole the car!

I was shown to a table by a waitress as sweet as they come, and with a charming pink-white skin and soft eyes that would have seduced a confirmed homosexual! I studied the menu card yet couldn't understand it. I selected a plateful of creamy cakes designed to ease my frustration or take revenge on my husband, or both. I can't explain it really. My mouth positively drooling, I began tucking in, when a chair nearby fell over and made us all jump. It had been knocked over by a stout dignified kind of man, the sort I tend to day-dream about, and he was proferring apologies to us all in German. He was tall when he stretched to his full height, with brown hair, wearing casual clothes. However, what impressed me were his hand movements, so controlled and gentle. I watched fascinated, thinking perversely how nice it would be to have them running over my body. Our eyes met as I glanced furtively at his face, and I quickly finished my cakes, suddenly finding them difficult to swallow.

Outside on the pavement I realized it had become night. It was much colder and there were few people about. I hurried to the car, scuffling in my bag for the keys. I dropped them and was getting into quite a state when a man's deep friendly voice made me spin round. Across the language barrier the coffee house man offered to open the car door for me. I smiled weakly and he beamed back at me. There was some confusion while we sought a common language, which turned out to be French, then he asked if I should like him to take the wheel. To which I said yes, as if it was the most natural thing in the world. As we conversed haltingly, I told myself I was being completely crazy, but then remembered the awful people I would have to spend the evening with. Why was I going with this man? Why not, if it came to that? It was the chance of a lifetime.

Ludwig gabbled away, telling me about the hotels and monuments and squares as we passed. And the more he went on, the more I smiled and shifted in my seat. I could feel myself becoming more radiant and sensual as the minutes went by. In the end I told him I was so glad we had met, and that he was exactly my type. He flashed his teeth at me and I blushed.

On and on we went, pulling up at last in front of a suburban timber house. He kept the car keys and took me inside. The inebriating fragrance of a log fire struck me instantly. We sat on a sofa side by side in front of the fire with a disc of Wagnerian overtures providing background music. Ludwig poured me orange juice, and told me about his childhood spent in poverty and his parents who were killed together in a car crash. I don't know how much of his yarn was true, but I just gaped at him with parted lips, willing to believe anything as long as he was going to take me in his arms. From time to time I laid a hand on his arm in commiseration, but he went droning on for a whole hour, while I squirmed about getting more and more disconcerted. I don't think I had ever wanted a man so much in my whole life!

At last he took my hands in his, and without further preliminaries led me upstairs where he undressed me expertly and pulled back the bedclothes. We made love hesitantly at first and then with animal fierceness. He was so strong and manly and silent! A blissful change from my idiot of a husband with his vulgar little perversions

117

inspired from dirty books he reads in secret but never shows me. Ludwig was a real man and knew what a woman wanted, especially one who was crying out for fulfilment.

Ignoring the punishment that awaited me, I stayed the night, and next morning we breakfasted dreamily in the Viennese style, punctuated by much kissing and fond caresses.

The moment to separate arrived. Ludwig said we must see each other again, and I said I'd cross the world to find him. He started the car and warmed up the engine for me, then got out with a final kiss.

I knew when I saw my husband pacing the hotel foyer that the end of the world was nigh. I told him a tale about meeting a woman I knew who had no telephone, then haughtily informed him I had a headache and was going to bed.

I snuggled luxuriously into the bed as naked as the day I was born, and thought about Ludwig and the ways we had made love. I wished he was right there with me, so that we could do it some more. I could have made love with him for a week!

Around two o'clock I got up, had a shower then took my time dressing and making-up. Downstairs a phone message was waiting for me. I was to come to the villa. I took a taxi at once!

He was talking with his parrot when I arrived, making it repeat the word Malika – my name! He had the fire going and we made for the sofa, kissing and fondling each other. Within 10 minutes we were upstairs frantically removing the last of our clothes, and plunging into an orgy of love-making.

When it was over we gazed into each others' eyes, declaring our eternal love.

The next day my husband took me home. I shall remember Ludwig till the day I die.

Malika K.

BODY SMILES

A Wonder Of Colour

Clarisse drove the hour's journey to the station in her white Rodeo, and settled into her seat in the Corail train to Paris-Saint-Lazare, excited as a little girl returning home from boarding school.

She and her husband lived in a hamlet with no station, no bus service, no grocer shop, no anything. It was simplest to drive to the nearest town and take the train for Paris. Clarisse read a few pages from her book on irises, flowers being a great interest to her, feeling particularly pleased with life on that sunny morning. Then there were railway lines to left and right, and the points made a noise, so she knew they were only a few minutes from the terminus.

As so many times in the past, she stepped lightly from the train, tripped neatly down the platform, and through the main hall, heading for the Boulevard des Italiens. It was a ritual, two days every month to do the art galleries. She loved painting above everything. She herself was an engraver and her husband a specialist in oils. In their early teens they had both known what they wanted to be, then a few years after that they met at the Ecole des Beaux-Arts, and were married a month later. They had been together for 13 contented and fruitful years.

On this lovely morning she scorned the Metro, preferring the short bus trip, so that she could drink in the colours and shapes of the streets, the shops, the trees, the avenues, the street vendors and the art dealers. Then she changed her mind and walked, knowing the voluptuous joy of sighting a square, a bridge or a boulevard from a distance and gradually getting nearer so that the perspective diminished to nothing. She had always had an attractive walk, her limbs swinging from the waist confidently though not too fast, her hips swaying gently as her skirt swirled left and right by just the right amount – so her husband had told her more than once. Today she wore an almost weightless dress with a low neckline. Her supple, upright bearing she owed to 11 years of classical dance classes. From an early age she had realized that a healthy mind stemmed from knowledge of what one's body could or could not do. Even these days she played tennis, went skiing and rambling to offset the sedentary nature of her work. She swam, too, whenever she could, and liked dancing whenever she got the chance; these were the two activities that gave her most satisfaction. In a word, at 35 the world was still her oyster.

A cup of coffee? Why ever not! Clarisse stopped at one of the nondescript modern places and picked a little round table outside, where she ran over her plans. Today she would do the Cezanne show, call in at the Avenue Matignon galleries, then cross over to the Latin Quarter and see what Claude Bernard had to show. And of course there was the Paris-Rome-Athens event. Around eight o'clock she would meet her friends for a film, followed by a meal at a Chinese restaurant. They would put her up for the night. As Clarisse sat musing, the sun filtered from one side through her profuse black hair and warmed her neck. She felt pretty and at ease with the world. Tomorrow she would see the Braque collages at the Pompidou Centre and the Nikkon Gallery photos a few yards away. She hoped she could do everything, not like last time when she had had to rush for the train back. Anyhow, the next stop was Cezanne.

She left a coin on the table, threw her bag over her shoulder, got up and checked she hadn't forgotten her cigarettes and lighter, and smiled at the *garcon* – as parisian as they make them in his black trousers and wine-hued jacket.

Mercifully there were relatively few people at the Grand Palais, mostly foreign tourists she noticed as she mounted the steps. A few minutes after eleven and she was slipping her ticket into her wallet, firmly snapping shut her large black bag. She joined the short line of people waiting to go in. It would be pleasant having plenty of room to view the pictures, nice too in such a light dress.

There was some fuss ahead about letting a student in, and she idly turned round to find a pair of limpid blue eyes looking straight into hers. She froze, unable to move or lower her eyes or even breathe. She was transfixed! And so apparently was the owner of the eyes. They simply stood facing each other in wonder. Clarisse shivered and after long seconds blurted out 'Do you like Cezanne?' And then smiled at the man. Confused, she turned round as the line of people shuffled forward. Together they moved into the first room. Petrified but with her heart pounding, she kept her head down, reliving the swift scene, seeing the large blue eyes in the man's sensitive, handsome face. He had not replied, and she pulled herself together.

'I paint,' he said simply. She looked up and saw he was wearing red canvas trousers, a sky blue shirt and a red sweater slung over his shoulders. How amazing that he, too, should paint! Clarisse felt a shiver rise up her backbone. 'My name's Christian. Yes, I adore Cezanne and I think I shall even more from today.'

They went to the first painting, a self-portrait with the head facing left and the paint not covering the whole canvas. The glass seemed to cut her off from the portrait. The man was close to her, and they both leaned forward to study the brush technique, the colour juxtapositions. She felt wisps of their hair touching and wondered if he did, and when they leaned back again they smiled at each other. She was perfectly calm now, breathing naturally, and she took a couple of steps to the next exhibit, another in oils, of the painter's wife seated in a garden with her elbows on a table. Christian moved next to her. Neither of them spoke, Clarisse frowned at the colour renderings. One by one the paintings went by, and she had a feeling of sensual complicity between their bodies and with the paintings. In *Le Parc De Chateau-Noir*, it was the tonal contrast that struck her, the ochre of the rocks challenging the green foliage, the varied blues, greens and yellows applied by means of fine brush strokes. Clarisse's pores opened to absorb the glow of the light and shade, the exciting atmosphere. Then they got to *La Montagne Sainte-Victoire*: trees, undergrowth, and the slopes beyond between the plain and the mountain range in the distance. It was quite magical, and Clarisse felt Christian's warm hand close round her own. Together they strolled through the woods, imbibing the intimacy of the scene, just the two of them.

She turned to face him, just as he moved and their bodies touched. The vibrations from the colours leaped out at her as she saw the vortex of desire in his eyes. Christian ran a hand over her shoulders, extended a warm caress to her exposed skin, confidently and gently drawing her to him until his mouth was on hers, but only for a second or two. She pushed her lips forward to speak, but this time the kiss lasted and spread, as they gave themselves up to the electric contact. A delicious tingle rose from her neck and his lips were tugging at hers, moist and soft. She pulled away first and looked at the distant mountains, seeing the sky come alive. The kiss had confirmed the mutual attraction in their eyes, and Clarisse felt herself go pale, sinking into the canvas. Christian undid the top button on the front of her dress, then the next and the others until the last came away and the dress fell from her back leaving her practically naked in her tiny knickers, her hips still golden from the summer. The couple lay down on the ground where the colours were most vivid, merging into the landscape, the undergrowth. She helped him take his clothes off and he removed her remaining garment. Their nakedness con-, trasted with the wispy blues, greens and the ochre that made everything so limpid.

Her breasts rose and fell with her breathing, as they gazed longingly at each other lubriciously and with mounting impatience. The infinite variety of the light as it played around them enhanced the colours, making the moment richer, and she fought to capture the paroxysm of each second. She had never been able to compartmentalize her body and her emotions; for her, the more harmony between two bodies the more intense the love. Now Christian was caressing her pelvis, in a triangular movement as irregular as Sainte-Victoire mountain. The dark thatch of her pubis spread over her white thighs, and her eyes sought his in adoration, plunging into the grave immensity of his blue pupils. A force from her entrails surged through her, and she drew him down on her, saying 'Now!' Christian was shaking as he enfolded her, one hand under her black tresses, the other lifting her body. He entered her and they heaved back and forth, choking for breath as their lust for each other grew more urgent. Clarisse perceived two trees high above them and felt their hard roots under her. Happy, ecstatic, she offered herself to the male, falling in with his rhythm, until she no longer felt the dead leaves and twigs making weals on her bottom and back. Her climax was near and this brought it on quicker. Christian grunted, forcing his mouth onto hers, snarling into her. Then she threw her head back in abandon and she came mightily as he swelled and burst within her. They were a single human tribute to the mountain, replete with beauty and truth. Nature had surrounded them and they impregnated it, the harsh soil of Provence soaked with the palpitations of two beings who had become colour, light, substance. 'When colour is at its richest, form is at its height,' so she had learned at the Beaux-Arts.

Clarisse remained still a long time on the ground, before opening her eyes in response to Christian's post-coital touches. She stretched and squirmed like a cat, and said 'Mmmm ...' Swimming in the green paradise, she strove to convey to him the charm, the mystery, the sweetness of this blissful minute. She convinced herself that he felt it too. To give herself the courage to speak, she lay her head on his chest and admired the haunches and long muscled legs of the body she found so beautiful.

Clinging to him, she said simply: 'Thankyou.'

He whispered: 'Look at me again like you did before.' He was overcome, pulling her to him, feeling the full flesh of her woman's body. With passion they had burst forth in a living bouquet, and now they looked at the mountain together, its subtle colourings against the half-tones of the undergrowth, its concaves, convexes, verticals and horizontals. A wonder of colour held steady in space.

Christian helped her up. She had no comb with her, but it was of no consequences. As she meekly buttoned up her dress, she could not take her eyes off him, appraising his shoulders and the firm muscles, seeing his great back for the first time, finding a nobility to it. His red clothes softened the blues of the undergrowth.

Their thighs touching, hand in hand they skipped towards the mountain, laughing at the criss-cross of colours under their feet. Christian stopped and bent down, collecting a blend of blue and orange for her, which she massaged into her hair and heart. Eventually they came out into a bare flat dull area. It was made up of squares, regularly disposed.

'How did we ...?'

'Look,' she said. 'Up there higher. That's where the picture is, on the wall.'

The journey into the canvas was over. They continued their visit, seeing exactly 47 more items. At one point they agreed: 'At the instant of painting, Cezanne composes what he sees with what he has seen and what he might see.'

An hour later, they slowly descended the steps outside the Grand Palais, the happiest couple in Paris that day.

'Clarisse,' he said, 'when shall we meet again?'

'Never.'

'Why?'

'So that I never lose you.'

Marie Ambre

Do Not Touch

He was well into his subject, accompanied by his usual gestures, rattling on about the latest guff in *Le Monde*, about fascism, about how they all came to meet.

That day, for some reason she could never identify, she was hypnotized by the pale transparent skin of his hand, the visible pulsing in the purple veins. Her eyes bore into the hand which dangled loosely on the arm of the fawn leather chair. Her own blood seemed to run faster through her veins, the more so since she was terrified he would look at her, noticing her sexual ferment. Then, when the meeting broke up, he said 'See you tomorrow?' as usual, and she smiled a smile that would have melted a granite statue.

And the next but one morning: 'Hullo there, you look fresh as a daisy. Sleep well?'

'Yes I did, actually, dreamed a lot too ...'

Yes indeed, I dreamed of you, a nice sexy dream that told me all about your chest, how it crushed my bosom, how your hip bones dug in as your springy flat abdomen pressed against mine and how you flooded me with your thick hot spunk ...

'You look ravishing. New hair-do?'

She always wore her hair carefully drawn back to form an array of intertwined, knotted, rolled tresses that were held in position by pins and small combs in tortoise-shell and mother-of-pearl. Last night she washed it and now a thousand micro-thin wisps were sparkling as they escaped the knots and rolls.

One moment, Eva, go down into a lotus-position, so that I can rub myself against your cool back, bite your shapely neck, place my legs on either side of your body, imprison your arms. I want to remove those pins one by one, just like they remove the stitches at the clinic. I'll gently unloose the strands of your hair and at last let your magnificent copper glory descend and the henna fragrance will fill my nostrils. And then, what joy, those silken waves will swirl around my cock!

So that's why you are suddenly interested in my hair style. True, I've done it rather differently this morning, but you do have a cheek, you know.

She had always liked these little ballet steps round the altar of love, in which he is allowed to approach her but may not touch. A dance of promise and nuances, stifling the burning fever which enflames his loins and tells him he must have her quickly. A game of hoped-for caresses, of dreams and longings.

Last night, she had gone to the Forum, where the central markets used to be. It was her first visit there, to a maze of underground alleys, people like zombies criss-crossing with other zombies, robots advancing to the mechanical clink of money, paying for the car park mechanically ... The cops seemed to be the only human-looking adjuncts to the place. The world had turned upside down!

'Yes, I agree, all those remote-controlled crowds make you think. In my country they kill and torture, and I left it all with no regrets, with a total lucidity, despite the very real danger, almost without a risk. But here, in places like that I tend to get scared, and the problem's worse every day.'

Oh my God, I'm starting again! Just as you turned to face me on the word 'scared', for the first time I caught the fresh spicy aroma of your breath, free of tobacco. How I would love to caress those dry open lips of yours and savour their lush firmness.

But neither of them moved. They simply stayed there in trepidation.

Two days later he exclaimed: 'Oh I do like those colours, Eva, they suit you perfectly!'

The red of her mohair jumper made a perfect match with the lipstick gloss of lips. He stared at her eyes, the jumper, her mouth, and her jumper again. He flushed imperceptibly but she had noticed, he stammered as he went on, his temples throbbing. Blood rushed round his head, as he thought of the blood in her lips, the blood coursing through his veins, stiffening his cock.

He was saying: ' ... it was just before the whole thing

blew up. It's terrible, I can never go back, I had to abandon my family, a good career, father, grandfather. But I don't know why I'm telling you all this!'

This time terror invaded his face. She saw delicate, beautiful-manicured nails, – intellectual's hands that could never kill. She saw the waxy pallour of his brow, and in his black pupils she read an appeal for life.

You frighten me and I yearn to nurse you, your head on my stomach. I flee and you bar the way, you escape and I seek you out. One word, just one, and everything would become possible, everything would tilt. But which word?

Later she found him deep in *Le Monde*, his countenance serious and grave with suffering, and she dared not go near him.

She's there, I can feel her presence.

'Goodnight, then. You look worn out.'

'I am indeed.'

And I'm exasperated by his coldness, a bulldozer is shovelling earth within me, ripping a path through my flesh. So you are afraid, sir, and you are buried in *Le Monde*. What kind of game are you playing?

'If ever there is a war, I don't think I could fight and join the partisans again. In any case, the cobblestones weren't the same as bombs and guns. I imagine I would bend double like a she-wolf, clutching my young to me, fleeing like a beast!'

'You'll be here tomorrow?'

'With pleasure – perhaps ...'

Eva Gange

Three Little Piggies

Of course I'm not a nice girl at all. For example, on the night in question I went into the bathroom at my friends' place where they had the party, and straddled the toilet and pissed all over my hands, just to feel the warmth coming out of my body. And was it hot!

Afterwards I went to my car and drove off under the new moon, alone in the universe on the motorway.

At least, that's what I thought until these three mobike cops forced me onto the hard shoulder and informed me that, back in Paris, I had gone through three red lights. And when it comes to cops you can't get much naughtier than that.

At least, that's what I thought! But I'm getting ahead of myself, because first they wanted to see all my documents and I fished them out as best I could including a photo of a man's chopper, a real work of art showing the veins and everything, so you could almost see the juice creeping up to that tiny hole at the end. Well, as they were leaning over taking a good look at my tits and knees – a girl is so vulnerable in a car – I explained that I'd had rather a lot to drink because it was the new moon, and since I'd had the luck to be stopped by three handsome guys could they possibly see me home? I'd give them all a big kiss if they did. I kept smiling at them and I guess I was grinning from ear to ear because of the whisky and because I was feeling as randy as hell anyway. Would they please, please see me home? Well, a man's a man however he's togged up, and as it was their time for going off duty they said they would. Yippee! So we went off at a careful 70 miles an hour with me driving the car, a cop in front and two others behind. I felt like the Queen of Sheba and reckoned I could keep going like that for ever.

The closer we got to my place the more I felt like crying on their shoulders. We went under the bridge, along an avenue and there was my gateway all lit up. We all came to a halt then, and I pulled up my skirt a bit and got out, telling my guardian angels they couldn't leave me now, but would they kindly switch off their engines so the neighbours wouldn't wake up. I went on for about five minutes, touching them and telling them they were really sweet to bring me home like that and, as they were off-duty, what about coming up for a drink? I had some excellent brandy and it would warm them up nicely – and a more obvious double meaning they'd never hear!

So they hid their bikes and I took them into the lounge which is also my bedroom. The brandy bottle was three-quarters full, which was a stroke of luck, and I poured out four glasses and sat my three boys down opposite a photo on the wall showing me in the style of West Side Story, hands on hips, legs apart and my mound of Venus openly on view. The fact that I was naked in the picture added to the interest, and I was hoping they'd say something if only that it was artistic. I relieved them of their crash helmets and hid them away so they couldn't leave in a rush, then removed an article of clothing – my overcoat. To ease the tension I flipped open the top three buttons of my blouse, telling the lads it was one button for each of them. After which I said they might as well see what was underneath while they were there and I undid the other three, so that the garment in question came away and displayed my two lovely boobs. I stretched and rubbed them against their three leather jackets in turn, and by the time the third man had choked on his brandy my nipples were sticking out like a couple of milk-filled teats on a baby's bottle.

My admirers took a sip at their juice and waited for the next item on the programme. I gave them a neat little wriggle or two while I divested myself of the only article of clothing that really counts on these occasions. I did an about-turn, slid my dress up higher and higher and higher, then backed towards them and bent over to show each of them my full moon. I was beginning to think they had drink but no drive and I ought to phone a rent-a-lover, when I heard a lustful moan and a couple of hands grasped the succulent flesh of my nether cheeks. A third hand slid up the backs of my thighs and introduced a duo of fingers into my cunt. This hand I held onto and rotated my willowy body, in order to shake hands with the owner's truncheon. I unzipped him and gave his prick and undercarriage an airing. He was a nice fat fellow and had a smile at the corners of his mouth he didn't know what to do with. He tried to get my mouth on his weapon, but I quickly shifted to the next man, shoving my knee in his crotch and my hand in his underpants. They don't teach you that at the yoga school, but the effect on number two was electric. The third man had got the message by now; he already had his tool out, and was fingering it vigorously.

It was seeing this that drove me wild. I thawed like a fruit from a deep freezer and parked myself on the very edge of my table, legs splayed and jerking myself off frantically, my right hand vibrating my clit and two fingers of the other hand in my back passage. Seeing the juice trickling from me, the three musketeers moved forward as one with the firm intention of coming in at the kill. Sure, I could have accommodated them simul-taneously, but I had other ideas buzzing around in my head: viz, to watch them do it to each other! Just like the three little piggies!!!

I stopped masturbating and took a blond wig of mine from a drawer, which I jammed between my legs to save wetting the carpet. Then I went to the oldest cop, who had a mustache and slowly undressed him, taking everything off and pulling his legs apart, so that I could lick his arse, pushing my quivering tongue in as far as I could, followed by a finger. Meanwhile I was wanking the youngest fellow with my other hand, occasionally abandoning the oldster and spitting on the youngster's taut stem. When this was shining with saliva and he was clearly ready to shoot, I offered him the other's backside, which he entered with all the enthusiasm of a centre-forward scoring the winning goal of the match.

I left them to it, and turned to the third cop, massaging his marbles and transferring his prick from his hand to my mouth. I was in my element, giving him little flicks and sucking him with such strength that spittle was swamping my chin. The other two were going like steam engines, the 'female' bent over a chair-back, the other hauling him back and forth on his big pole. At this juncture, to coin a phrase, I gradually led my third man over, jerking him as fast as I could, so that his business end was opposite the mustache. I squeezed him a second or two, feeling his gland swell and tremble, then let it go – and so did he! Right into the face of grand-dad just as he was opening his mouth to protest!

The sight was so thrilling that I plunged my two hands into the wig wedged into my sopping crotch and brought myself off in seconds. We were panting like a herd of elephants, as the Vatican so knowingly put it on one noted occasion, and we collapsed writhing with laughter in a heap.

It was then that I caught sight of the new moon shining through the window.

'Look boys,' I said, 'she's smiling at you. I bet she enjoyed the performance as much as I.'

Sylviane Gouirand

PUNISHMENT

Champagne For Lunch

How could I have displeased you? I agree the things I said were silly, and you ought not to have taken any notice. Perhaps I don't really know you and you're a Don Juan? A girl for every day? But maybe those excesses were repeated with each woman, with the same vigour and violence, so that they were all treated alike! I don't know what to think, I'm unable to account for your silence, unable to explain it.

Beauty had been my pointless companion day by day, I have regained the purity of my curves, my face has been transfigured! But this had inevitably given way to a decline as I try to return to the state I was in before meeting you. Not that I love you. When I paid you a courtesy call that day, which I owed you, I arrived in a rather bored mood, not looking forward to the small talk needed when one knows little of the other's tastes. I found little to say, was circumspect, embarrassed, intimidated.

At midday you suggested champagne, and as it is my preferred drink I accepted without hesitation. I drink a lot of it, and I supposed you did too. I saw no special reason why your champagne should make me over-excited, and looking back I hate you for it. If you were to invite me again, I wonder if you'd open some more for me, now that you know I am willing to do anything, which was something I had forgotten when I called.

Thus we had champagne and small talk about our various plans, houses we'd lived in, common friends. You seemed as shy as I was. You had phoned me to say thankyou for my little note about the party one of our friends took me to, and in view of your silence I ought not to have prejudiced your timidity and hurried you by suggesting a meeting. It was a mistake. Perhaps we had nothing to say to each other, I thought.

Then you said we must have a bite to eat, and you got a tray done with ham and things. Whereupon we went into another room in the oriental style, but with no champagne.

When we got there, your countenance changed out of all recognition. You suddenly got out your penis, forced my legs apart and masturbated for all you were worth, staring under my skirt. Naturally I could do nothing about it, and merely supposed that you were a *voyeur*. I endeavoured to recover my poise, but you found a riding whip behind a cushion and handed it to me. You took your trousers down and presented your hind quarters to me, while you looked into that mirror. To be frank, I wanted to laugh more at your position with your haunches exposed, rather than your use of the mirror in that way.

I whipped you as hard as I could, that being the first time I had done such a thing. Then I found I liked it and beat you frantically, getting a thrill out of it. Afterwards you turned round and masturbated again with your thing a few inches from my own sex. I refused to let you come nearer, poking the whip in your pelvis, I was convinced I was right, for either you were a *voyeur* or you liked to be thrashed, or both, but I was not going to let you reverse the roles and take me as a woman, legs up and all! And yet that is exactly what happened, and it was my turn to consent, to submit gaily, so to speak, to the classic role. I was pleasantly surprised, having assumed there was no question of that. In the event I let you take me from behind, I reached my climax and lay back exhausted on the carpet.

As we recovered and I gazed at the ceiling I gave my fantasies free rein: erotic thoughts, pornographic thoughts, all in the manner of a farce. But after a while these mental meanderings became rather frightening, and I sought another diversion, if possible chic and fun. Something for 'after lunch', as it were!

We got up and sat on the sofa, where your hand sidled between my legs and rubbed me expertly. I pushed you away to start with, but found I wanted to have it again. You brought me to a second climax, and being in an awfully unladylike position I blushed with shame. Then I day-dreamed of this and that until you put the carpet right and I assumed you wanted me to leave. In fact you suggested we got out for a coffee somewhere, and I imagined this was to be the polite dismissal. But I stayed put, asking stupid questions in an attempt to wake myself up: 'Does this happen every afternoon? Do you have lunch like this every day?' My curious behaviour was due, I supposed, to the chmpagne and the weed from your garden which we smoked. You began talking about your solitude in the country where you did your writing, and your austere existence, and finally declared that 'something had changed today'.

I got ready at last, and we went down. On the pavement outside you offered me your arm saying: 'It's really rather pleasant this light effect, similar to Rome in September, don't you feel?' We had our coffee and said goodbye, embracing fast on the cheek like the good friends we were.

And I haven't heard a word since. In what way did I displease you? Have you died a violent death?

I think you are being very shallow. Surely you must realize what fun we could have together, have you thought of that? At times I tell myself the angels are looking after me, that you are the devil and would have led me into hopeless debauchery, from which I have miraculously escaped. At other times I flush with shame at what I must have looked like. Or again I am scared at the violence of our encounter. Perhaps it is because you know I would let you do absolutely anything with me, that you lost interest. I was on a plate. I can understand that. Even so let me assure you it was the first time I had ever done such things in my life, although I agree I seemed to be making up for lost time!

What do you expect me to do now, may I ask? I make this appeal even though you have become quite repulsive to me. You could at least have sent a few flowers the next day, written a little compliment. But nothing! Unless of course you are one of those people who like instant excesses and then turn the page.

We shall bump into each other again at some show, or an art exhibition, at some friends' houses. You can't get away with a mere 'How are you?' You can go to the devil. I hate you. When I think of your absurd little bottom, out of some boulevard farce, I find you grotesque. God preserve me from another encounter with you, and I hope I never see you again. I am furious that you made me lose control like that, and wish my father would give you what you deserve. You ought to be guillotined for it, that's what you warrant! For making me mad, reducing me to an idiot screwing up her hands in distress.

When I called on you I assure you my intention was to ignore my age and let my hair grow white without dyeing it, to rip out my false teeth and become old with dignity. And now you have turned me into a writhing, completely frustrated animal. I shall never forgive you, for I shall never find a lover in your category, no male to take me out of myself as you did. I am a shellfish naked on the burning sand, wondering who you are, who I am and what came over me.

You could have called me 'My Life', but you are incapable of love. Yes, one day in the comfort of some obscure library which I shuffle into, draped in black, you may yet look up from your book, gaze into my eyes and say: 'My Life.'

Seda

The Blockhouse

Over the loudspeaker came the announcement: 'Passengers are advised that we shall be arriving at L ... a few minutes from now.' At the same time the train began slowing.

She got up from her window. The man was still looking at her and she made a discreet sign to him as she squeezed past. He got up to follow and as she reached the sliding door she pointed to her suitcase. He nodded. She held her overcoat tight about her, and suddenly noticed that another man, seated, was staring straight ahead at her, glaring at the black stockings showing through a gaping slit in the coat. It was too late to do anything about it, even if he had caught a glimpse of the start of her shaven crack, so she just glowered back at him and went off farther down the coach.

At M ... a student slunk into her new compartment and sat next to her, pulling out a paperback. He started reading at once and she observed his hands through narrowed eyes. She wondered how he would react if she pushed her shoe against his. She hesitated, thinking of A who was waiting for her at the other end; she had forgotten to ask over the phone whether she could have a little fun of her own on the way, even if it meant she would be punished more harshly. She wavered only two or three seconds, saying that she liked being punished anyhow. She was proud of being a masochist; she would never be short of company! Her foot inched sideways and touched the youth's. He was startled, then his eyes sparkled when he realized this attractive woman was actually interested in him. She smiled at him, took out a ballpoint pen, and wrote inside the book: 'Follow me to the end.' She duly rose and went out. The student's eyes darted about fearfully, then he jumped up quickly. He found her already inside, wearing only a waspie type corset, the stockings and nothing else under the coat. She welcomed him in the toilet and closed the door again. Then the woman gently took his head in her hands, gave him a kiss, and pulled down his trouser zip. She had to push herself forward in front so that he could penetrate her, but once this was achieved they rocked until they both had their pleasure in turn. Then she went back to her seat in the compartment, and demurely crossed her legs under the folds of her coat.

At R ... the student left the train and was replaced by a teacher who sat with a pile of homework on flowers and pollen. He began correcting them, but within minutes his eyes strayed to the woman's knees, now showing appetizingly as she dozed with the coat falling away a little. Deftly he slid his hand under the coat, she uncrossed her knees and parted them slightly. He whispered: 'You can have me,' as he rolled his head round towards her ear with every appearance of a natural movement. At the same moment she got her hand under the homework and felt him; his member was hard. It was a matter of a minute, no longer, before she unzipped him and had his warm sperm wetting her fingers. She opened her eyes as he came and smiled at his flushed face and attempts to breath normally.

The next station was hers, and once on the platform she accepted her case from the teacher, who gave a tiny wave and resumed his seat.

As nobody appeared to be on the look-out for her, she walked out to the station concourse. She stood for an instant and heard a car door slam; a man came over and asked her if she was the lady for Les Mouettes. She said yes and he took her case, placing it in the back of the car. She took her place behind the chauffeur, and stared at his neck as they swiftly emerged from the town. It was as closely shaved as her own pubis, she thought. She slipped her hand under her coat to feel her warm soft quim. This she began caressing with her eyes closed, thinking of her own chauffeur who had made love to her on the backseat after a race meeting not two weeks earlier. Unwittingly, she released a few whimpering noises as she neared her climax and the chauffeur braked suddenly, so that she hit her mouth on the seat in front. He nipped out and opened the door, pulling her by the arm, rushing her forcefully into a copse by the road. He strode along and she had to run to keep up.

'Get down on your knees,' he ordered about 50 yards from the road. There was no disobeying the timbre of his voice, and she squatted down, the pine needles hurting her. 'Bend over,' the man ordered.

He drew back her coat, and she wriggled excitedly, imagining her well-filled bottom exposed to him like a mare's. She heard him clumping around and was intrigued, but dared not move. Then suddenly there was a 'whoip' sound and she felt the sting of a stick on her bottom. He gave her half a dozen strokes, and she lived each one of them from start to finish, not making a sound. Then she heard him taking his trousers down and cried 'No, no! but he grabbed her waist. She liked to hear herself protesting. He poked her roughly, grunted his pleasure, and then helped her up. She had not come, and enjoyed that humiliation too.

'Do your hair,' he said, handing her a comb. She did as she was told, and joined him in the car. 'Your train was late, we must hurry now,' he informed her.

The road was none too smooth, and she lifted up the back of her coat, squashing her bottom into the leather upholstery, feeling the burn from the thrashing. She looked at the pine trees, wondering if they would come back, and whether he might chain her to a tree, thrashing her again. The car turned into a drive past a pair of large gates, its tyres crunching. They pulled up outside an austere residence with white paintwork, where a woman in black came out. The woman was in her 30s and came up to the car window.

'Monsieur is waiting for you in his study,' she said.

The visitor breathed in the pungent smell of earth and trees as she followed the woman into the main hall, where she turned and inspected the newcomer. She shivered as she realized there might be some leaves still stuck to her coat, or some pine needles.

'What have you done with your boots?' said the other woman. 'They are dirty, like some peasant who's been through the woods. Take them off, and put your shoes on.'

The chauffeur had left the suitcase, and she knelt down meekly to take her shoes out: high-heeled court shoes, with a strap that went round her ankle. She was taken into the study, where A was on the phone. The door closed behind her, and she stood motionless, not daring to move forward or sit in a vacant armchair. She kept her eyes lowered.

There was no going back now, once she had agreed to come down. She had found out his tastes since they first met a month ago at the gallery she ran; she knew he insisted on being the complete master. She had been impressed by his fierce blue eyes and his manner of broaching the subject; he had appreciated her discretion from the outset. A had asked her to put a nude painting by for him, then one day just before closing time he had phoned.

'Good evening, this is A. Could you possibly bring that painting down on Wednesday around noon? I'm sure you'll say yes.'

'Yes of course, sir.'

'I'll give you until this time tomorrow to change your mind. I wish you to belong to me completely, and carry out my every command.'

He had repeated those last words and had rung off. She stayed with her hand on the receiver, her breath quickening. Did he want her as his slave, or as a call girl? Either way it was dangerous and she wished she had pulled out when she could. But the temptation was overwhelming, delicious: she would submit to every kind of punishment, every humiliation. They might even form a long-lasting partnership and she might fall in love with him – in her own way.

A put down the phone, making her jump. The man looked at her for a full minute, and she lowered her eyes again.

'Take your coat off.'

She did so and looked at him, sitting behind the desk in a black suit. The coat fell to the ground.

'Walk about,' he ordered.

He had a clipped voice, but it was soft somehow, controlled. She walked back and forth in front of the desk, the humiliation gripping her. The waspie corset pushed up her breasts, which were naked. She wore nothing below and felt his gaze on her hind quarters and her shaven quim. She would keep walking as long as he wished her to. He had asked her specially to come like that with the coat over the top.

'Come here,' he instructed. He ran a finger over the start of her rear crack. 'You were late because you stopped on the way?'

'Yes.'

'With whom?'

'Your chauffeur.'

She could easily have lied to him, but she was impatient now to belong to him.

'Hm. You allow yourself to be played around with by simply anyone! You are more flightly than I thought.' She said nothing, stayed still, feeling his hand lightly on her bottom. 'Have you ever been whipped before?'

'No.'

'You will be. But I shall take my time.'

The master of the house rose at last, went behind her and caught her arms, pulling them behind.

In a harsher voice he said: 'If you forget to keep them behind you, I shall have to use handcuffs.'

He pushed a button and the woman in black entered. He said: 'I want a very tight corset for her, so that she doesn't forget she is mine.' He put his arms round her waist. 'Your bosom and rump will be nicely offered to me!'

The host resumed his seat behind the desk, and she was led off to the room placed at her disposal. It was large, with a bed, a chest of drawers and a dressing table bearing a mirror system that showed the four corners of the room. The housekeeper drew near and undid the corset. The visitor was now fully naked, and the woman fingered her lips, her breasts and waist. She then pushed her down on the bed and spread her legs, forcing her firm tongue past her vulva, at the same time playing with herself between the legs. She then told her to get up, and said A wanted her to have a bath. The housekeeper fondled her again in the bath, and she submitted to this unpleasant assault from a creature who knew she could not object. On returning to the bedroom, the housekeeper pulled open a drawer full of black lace underwear, and selected a very small corset in real silk, forcing it round her victim. The wearer caught her breath at the pain, but refrained from crying out, although she would doubtless do so in A's presence. She studied herself in the mirrors, wide-eyed at her own jutting breasts and now-enormous bottom. She understood the pleasure this would give A. Stiffly, she squirmed about and put on new stockings. Then strutted about in them.

Suddenly A said from the bedroom doorway: 'You're taking an insufferably long time. You aren't afraid of me, are you?' Then to the other woman: 'Leave us.'

The man's hands came down on her shoulders: 'So, throughout your journey here, you were naughty. You must now take your punishment. Follow me!'

She kept her hands behind her, bouncing on her bulbous rear, and her eyes down. She walked behind him, rather piqued that he had made no remark about the tight corset. In the study A went to a cupboard and opened the twin doors; it was a kind of dressing area with mirrors all round, and overhead there was a horizontal bar. At the sight of this she instinctively tightened her legs. No doubt A would have liked to see the fright on her countenance.

He was saying: 'Before you arrived, I asked you to accept me as your complete master. While you are here I shall punish you as I wish, choosing my own time and place. Do you understand that?'

'Yes.'

'Yes, *master*.'

'Yes, master.'

From a drawer he extracted a metal necklace and thick handcuffs to match. He told her to sit on the edge of his desk, and as she took up this position he placed his legs either side of her.

'As you move about,' he explained, 'you will not set eyes on the chauffeur or the housekeeper or myself. I wish to see your eyes solely when I am inflicting punishment on you. I want to see the love in them, the pain and the hate, especially the hate.'

Her tormentor put a dog's collar round her neck so that the leash tickled her mound at the front. He knelt and clicked some fetters onto her ankles, with a short chain between them.

'This way, you will walk using tiny steps, and now give me your wrists.'

She did so, and he fixed the handcuffs, a short rope between them. Then A pulled her by means of the dog leash and she tottered along, feeling her bottom wobbling and the lips between her legs rubbing. She felt she would faint from the excitement, but A already had her under the horizontal bar and with the aid of some steps he attached her wrists to the bar, pulling so that she was on tiptoe. The pain was excruciating and she bit her tongue, she stopped herself crying because she was so happy being his slave. Even so she shut her eyes, and then heard A tapping a riding whip in his hand. The handcuffs dug into her wrists and she knew that even a whipping would be better than that. To humiliate her further. A asked her to decide how many she wanted.

'Five, yes, five strokes.'

He administered them, with a long pause between each. Then he sat down behind his desk. The pain in her wrists was unbearable, and she wanted to stamp on the ground but was unable to, wanted A to come to her rescue, to let her down.

'Another five minutes,' he said, enjoying the spectacle.

Then he let her down, and removed the various fetters. He rang for the housekeeper: 'Bring her the black dress.'

It was a dress with a slit up the side and no bodice, so that her breasts were exposed.

'Come now,' said A. 'We'll have lunch.' They went in to a table set for them both. 'We shall have lunch together, but this evening you will serve my meal.' When they had finished: 'You can go into my library until 5 o'clock, when you must fetch my coffee from the kitchen.'

'Yes, master.'

'But now, come over here.'

'Yes, master.'

She went round the table and he told her to pull up her

dress, turn around and bend over. He admired the weals on her bottom, and told her to go into his study for a moment. Once there, she saw the dressing area and the mirrors. She would have liked to see the marks too. This she did, feeling pleasure tingling within her as she saw the stripes, felt the ridges.

The master strode in: 'Lean over my desk and stretch your arms out.' In a single movement he lifted up the dress skirt, and gave her five more strokes with the riding whip. She stifled her cries, A pulled down the dress and told her to leave him.

In the library she selected a few books, but before settling down to read them she looked out of the window and saw a beach. She would have liked to run along the sand close to the shore, but even more she wanted to stay as a prisoner in the house, going out only with A's permission.

At 5 o'clock sharp, the other woman came in: 'You must take the coffee in now. The tray is in the kitchen.'

In the kitchen, the housekeeper slipped a hand in the dress slit, and forced her to open her legs, then thrust her fingers in the slave's vagina. The woman masturbated her until she had an orgasm, and then snarled: 'You whore!'

She took the tray in, and A was angry because she was 5 minutes late. He put his hand under her dress and masturbated her. She felt her vulva hot and viscous.

'Lick it off my hands, and now I must punish you for lateness. Take your dress off.' She was again solely in the tight corset. 'Go over to that corner, on your knees, arms raised.'

He put the handcuffs on and left her, drinking his coffee, putting in some phone calls, even writing some letters. Two hours went by without him glancing at her. Her arms ached terribly, and she was close to passing out when she became aware that he was rubbing his penis across her back.

'Give me your hands.' He removed the handcuffs. 'Open your mouth.'

He pushed his penis into her mouth and it hurt the back of her throat, he played there a while and then spurted inside her mouth. She swallowed the fluid.

'Thankyou, master,'she rasped.

'Go into the kitchen and get dinner ready.'

In the kitchen the chauffeur and housekeeper kept silent. The other woman gave her a basketful of vegetables to peel, then gave her her meal at the end of the kitchen table. Shortly before 8 o'clock the housekeeper gave her a white pinafore to go over the black dress. In the dining room the heavy blue velvet curtains were drawn, and A was seated at the table. Wordlessly, she laid his place, brought him his meal, cut his meat for him as he ordered, and poured out his wine.

At length he announced: 'An hour from now we shall take a stroll. Leave the dress here, the housekeeper will give you a cape.'

She served him coffee and went to her room, lay on her back and made love to herself, thinking of the pains and the humiliations of the day. With her other hand she felt the weals across her bottom from the master's whip. She had an orgasm and dozed off.

She woke to find her hand between her legs and the man looking down at her with a shocked expression: 'Whatever have you been doing?'

She flushed scarlet: 'I have been playing with myself.'

'Well, you'll certainly be punished for that, naughty girl!'

She followed him to the study with mincing steps, and A put the necklace on her. He put various fetters and chains in his pockets. They went outside and got in the car; he took the wheel and she sat beside him. She saw the outline of pine trees and these gave way to dunes. There he pulled up the car and she heard the sea lapping the shore. They got out and she walked behind him, keeping the cape tight round her, buffeted by a stiff breeze from the sea. They reached a blockhouse, and inside were blankets, while on one side was a pile of straw which A set fire to.

Taking the cape off, he said: 'Are you afraid?'

'Yes, master.'

'Do you know what I want to do with you?'

'No, master.'

'You are my bitch. Get on your knees!'

She did this and shivered with the cold and apprehension. This was a new phase, and she was scared. The man attached the dog leash to a ring, then fixed her wrists and ankles in such a way that she could move neither head, nor arms, nor legs. He blindfolded her and said she was powerless against him or anyone else who passed by. A she-dog, he said, already wetting itself with the fluid running down its thighs. She sensed him behind, and soon he was pulling her thighs apart. At last he mounted his bitch, and she fought to get free, the chains clanking and the shackles digging in. He forced her back down and penetrated her fiercely, bumping against her, venting his lust as he wished, telling her she was totally at his mercy. Afterwards he came to her side and stroked her cheek tenderly. It was the first affectionate gesture he had proferred.

'Thankyou, master,' she said. There was glee in his eyes.

'I'm leaving now. The chauffeur will fetch you.'

Panic seized her and she struggled to get free. He wouldn't leave her here alone, surely! The cape splayed over her back, and she heard him leave, the car start up and whine its way back to the house. Then all was silent, and the tears streamed down her cheeks and onto the ground.

She must have stayed like that, hopeless, for half an hour, having no notion of how long they would leave her. Then the car came back and she heard a man's steps. She was so happy, she didn't care who it was. The man entered and sat down behind her.

'What are you doing?' she said after a few seconds.

'Master's orders. You're to stay like that until morning. I'm just looking at you for a bit.'

'Oh no!'

'Keep quiet or I'll give it to you!'

After what seemed ages, the chauffeur's snores reached her ears. She herself was quite unable to sleep. She was too scared to speak.

The next morning he took the chains off, helped her up, put the cape on, and aided her as she staggered out. She was exhausted but she felt she was born again. Never had a morning seemed so sweet, calm and refreshingly beautiful!

At the house, all was quiet. She was served breakfast in her room, and allowed to take a bath. The housekeeper stayed with her, played with her once more.

Thus the first day and night went by.

Josephine L.

KISS OF DEATH

The Cross Of Love

I was asleep when he arrived. He turned the key in the door of my room, slipped it in his trouser pocket, and stood leaning against the foor frame. He smiled enchantingly, and at first sight appeared quite calm. Then I noticed an unnatural lustre to his eyes, and I watched him dozily with a certain forboding.

'Did I wake you?' There was irony in his voice. 'Well, the moment has come, it's now.'

I waded out of sleep at last, and remembered I hadn't closed the shutters, so that the brash music and gunshots from the permanent 'fair' drifted in from the Boulevard de Clichy. Enough light filtered in for us to see each other's features.

He stated quietly: 'Don't be afraid, I've come to set you free, free of me.'

He got out some thin nylon string, approached the bed, attached my arms and ankles behind my back.

'I want you to watch me die,' he said. At that point I didn't think he would go through with it, and I studied him as he looked down at the merry-go-rounds and firing ranges and other sideshows below. He smiled again and I was apprehensive.

'I'm madly in love with you,' he declared. He leaned back this time against one of the window uprights, his hands in his pockets. We looked at each other. 'Do you love me?' I knew I did not but I uttered no sound, so that he drew his own conclusions. 'In that case we'll do it right away.'

He lit a cigarette and smoked it slowly, blowing on the end at one stage and then crushing it into his palm. I thought I smelled the skin burning, and I felt sick.

'I'm cold,' I said. Wiping tears from his eyes he remarked: 'You're cold.' He felt my hatred and it seemed to console him. 'I love you, you are going to see me die and then you'll feel happy.'

It was some months since I had seen him, and I had been

happy without him, that was true. I had buried our love story and now I closed my eyes to make it go away again, listening to the noises from the street. For a few minutes I really imagined he had disappeared.

'Don't go to sleep, you've got to see me do it.'

I forced my eyes open and found he was lying down next to me. I detested him with all the emotion at my command. He felt the gut hate and chuckled: 'I could give you a baby right now. But I'll only make you witness my death.'

I thought he was still bragging. Especially as he set fire to another cigarette, which he waved over my stomach and then applied it to the skin on his hand, so that the same stink occurred and I shivered. I told him I was cold and he said he would begin. This made me furious, because I saw he was pleased at knowing I preferred him to die. I just wanted him to fire a bullet into his damned head and be done with it. He started blubbering, thinking how much he loved me no doubt.

Then I forgot the cord binding me, forgot he had come to kill himself, forgot my hate. Like a fool I felt sorry for him and realized my throat was thickening and the tears were on their way up. I managed to think about the facts, certain that he was crying simply to make me cry with him. I asked him to untie me, but he wiped his eyes and said no.

Why I had allowed myself to be bound in that way was hard to understand. He was not a violent man, he was gentle in spite of his piercing look. I supposed I was just too sleepy when he came in.

When we had first met more than 10 years back I told him I didn't believe in love. We were both at high school, of course.

Now he slid off the bed and sat hunched over at my desk, his back turned to me. It seemed to me that he had loved me solely because of my adolescent despair, and I mused that he had stolen 10 years of my life by loving me for that, I hated him. I imagined the funeral and I was sure I would be completely indifferent when they lowered him into the ground. Right then I was cold, I wanted to be left alone to go to sleep. Again I asked him to undo me and leave. He chuckled and said no. I was within an ace of telling him to hurry up and die, but restrained myself because that might make him drag it out longer. I shivered and wanted it over quick.

Turning to me he said: 'I am the keeper of your past suffering. When I go, so will all that.'

'You're out of your mind,' I said, without much conviction, knowing how determined he was. He must have watched me doze off, and I awoke because the noise outside came to an end. 'Come on, undo me and clear out.'

This time he agreed to untie me, but he stayed there, and I thought the compromise, that half-measure, was despicable, simply half giving in to me. He saw my contempt, his mouth twisted and I knew he wanted to hit me.

I slept a long time and woke late the next morning. He told me it was sunny and I turned to look at the window, noticing the sapphire sky. He sat on the bed and pushed his praying hands between his thighs, lowering his head like some penitent.

'Do you want me to open the door now?' he asked. I did not answer, and he got up and extracted the key and opened the bedroom door. I eased myself out of the bed and donned a bathrobe. He watched me from the vantage point of the doorway. Naturally I opened the window to let some air in, and looked down on the Boulevard de Clichy, in particular at the Pigalle Metro station steps with the *fin-de-siecle* ironwork over the top, the Morris pillar, the passers-by, the pigeons. I had no desire to discuss anything with him. I just wanted him to clear off.

Emerging from the bedroom I went down to the bathroom. For a moment I thought he'd gone, then I saw him on a bench thing next to the fireplace, flipping through a magazine, making himself quite at home. Without a word I ran a shower and stayed in it for ages, hoping he would go. I made some coffee just for myself but he joined me in the kitchen and found another cup.

'I shan't give it up, I'll go through with it, I dare you to watch me dying.' I found him sickening, eventually getting up and going to the French windows, pushing the curtain aside and looking out.

'Where are you going?' he snapped in an anguished tone. I looked round at him. He was still handsome but his face was drawn, fatigue lending his features the expression of a helpless little boy. He would burst out crying soon, I told myself. He had had that same expression 10 years earlier when I'd told him I was running out on him. The next day he cut his wrists, I was told, and I phoned him and we fixed up to meet. We had gone for a walk in the Parc de Saint Cloud, and a storm blew up. I could not say whether or not I really loved him, but I felt his attraction.

The cigarette burns showed clearly on his hands, and I thought that any normal person would hate him for behaving as he had done.

Suddenly I relented: 'Come on, we'll go for a walk and I'll show you where I used to live as a kid on the Butte Montmarte. We can stroll along the Canal Saint-Martin and the Seine if you like. We can look at the booksellers.'

So we walked down the alley lined with the Villa Frochot trees, then crossed Pigalle and on to the Place de Clichy, finally up to the Butte Montmartre. I enjoyed walking and wanted him to share that, but of course he had not slept. We had a coffee together on a *terrasse* outside Saint-Pierre church. I prattled on about the history lessons they gave us at the council school in Rue du Mont-Cenis. I mentioned the two Roman pillars inside the church, I told him about the Savoyarde which was a bell presented to the Sacre-Coeur basilica by the people in the Alps, describing how the bell brought the bridge down over the Montmartre cemetery and how the bell was cracked ever after. But he didn't listen, he was worn out. I glanced craftily at his profile and the bitter crease in his lips; I recalled that he had never in fact wanted to share my little pleasures. Later we went down the famous steps in the garden below the Sacre-Coeur, and I said I used to play there. I stopped and drank from the fountain; not that I was thirsty, for I simply wanted to push the metal knob and splash my lips, neck and feet.

Of course, I was trying to avoid thinking about last night, but to little effect. For example I imagined going to sleep and feeling an electric discharge in my inside, jumping at the very instant when he killed himself a few feet away.

I had said we could go along the canal but he was tired, miserable and obstinate. I would have liked to see the barges waiting to go through the lock, and the little iron bridges for pedestrians. We had gone there one winter's afternoon, and I had eaten shrimps as we walked. But he was weary and looking ashen, and I didn't want to go back to the Villa Frochot with him, knowing he needed sleep badly. I disliked the idea of him returning home with me, sensing his nastiness. This is what made me tell him; 'I'll leave you now.' He said nothing and I ran off, leaving him standing.

Weeks went by, and of course I had no intention of seeing or speaking to him. I was quite confident about it, and had pushed the whole thing out of my mind. Actually I was falling in love with someone else, and was thrilled about it. Friends mentioned him but I showed no interest. They said he was in a shocking state, not working, not eating, not even washing. I assumed he was trying to let himself die, which I judged a silly gesture. If only he would do what he said then I'd be rid of him! I had no conscience about it, affirming that anyone else would have adopted the same attitude. Nevertheless I asked a girl I knew if she had ever wished someone dead, and she said of course she had. Perhaps we would meet again in the next world, I said to myself, thinking our affair might turn out less hellish, although I would have preferred to lose contact for good.

When I went to sleep I used to imagine him coming in, right into my room and locking the door and going on about me watching him die and I would have to look at his suffering to free myself of my own suffering. I imagined a big festive occasion on the boulevard with a jangling of tunes and hucksters yelling over their loudspeakers. I imagined asking him if he was going to die that night, and him replying yes that night. I invented him choosing a slow poison because a slow one would let him display his suffering more cruelly. I saw him that night with a

159

countenance like Christ on the cross, and I was deeply repulsed, as intensely as he was suffering. Once I remembered that on our first Christmas together I bought him *Les Chants de Maldoror* when we were still at the lycee. I wrote in it; 'We are a pair of hermaphrodites stretching out to each other.' A few years later I reminded him of that gift, and he asserted that it was he who gave it to me and wrote in it. We got the book from the shelf and I recognized my own writing and he reckoned it was his. We had a row over it.

We seemed, as a couple, to be on the brink of madness all the time, and I had an inkling that I would leave him one day and become another person. Both of us accorded huge importance to the imagination, and we even called each other brother and sister. Undoubtedly we were drawn to each other because the most complete love is the most impossible love. We both knew and said nothing, sharing this basic intuition. Sometimes there was compassion between us, because we knew each others' despair. And occasionally we felt a wild tenderness. For 10 years we played at living together, and the first one who took it seriously was the one to be hurt. We fought brief, brutal battles with our bodies, sometimes using moral arguments as people do, but sometimes not. We knew our love-making would be sterile, that there would be no children. We each had our own secret lives, occasionally we were violently jealous, sometimes not; we had scenes over nothing like everybody else. Gradually I started to become that other person I mentioned, and I hoped he would too, but he was resolved to destroy me. One day I left him.

Then he came in as I was sleeping, turned the key in the door of my bedroom and tied me hand and foot behind my back. I let him do it because I knew he wanted to die in front of me when I was powerless. He told me he was the custodian of my drama and my sufferings. His death would free me, he said. I wasn't brave about it and I closed my eyes. 'I want you to watch me die,' he said. But I just wanted to scream and I didn't. I opened my eyes and said, 'Yes'. He lit a cigarette and smoked it slowly all the way. No, he did not burn his hand. I thought I would lack the courage to watch.

'It won't take long,' he whispered softly. So softly it was like a child speaking, and he had the gaze of a child, the awkward gestures of a child. He pulled a box from his pocket with a bottle inside and a syringe. 'I got it from a vet,' he muttered, 'it's for putting sick dogs to sleep.' I thought I would beseech him to share the poison with me, but I said nothing.

'It won't take long,' he repeated, 'but make sure you keep your eyes completely open.'

He filled the syringe, rolled up his sleeve, made a tourniquet with nylon string. The he jabbed a vein that was sticking up.

I was surprised how quickly it happened. He gave me a look, trying to tell me he was madly in love with me.

'No!!!' I shrieked.

But he nodded his head, meaning it was too late.

He gave me a last smile before his face began to contort, and I realized the immense hatred behind that final smile. His head flopped onto his chest and it was over.

By committing suicide in front of me, I believe he wanted to chain me irremediably to the cruellest of all sufferings.

Marguerite Arnaud

Devil In The Convent

It was the summer of 1940 and I was left at the convent during the main holiday, because of the war of course. It was scalding hot as I ambled round the grounds while the sisters were having their afternoon nap. There was no-one at the windows and I decided to take a look at the castle ruins; if I went behind the big pine tree I might be able to hop over the wall. I climbed up and managed to straddle the wall without giving myself away. I now had to jump down the other side, where there was a small earth path with a ditch. It was deserted and I had a moment's fear about how I could get back if the main gate was closed. I decided to stay where I was.

From the nearby town I heard a faint buzzing sound, it came nearer and became a motor noise, something never heard around the convent. It worried me. A score of motorcycles roared up ridden by men in black who looked dusty. Just my luck, they stopped and got off just below where I was sitting! I watched them take off their helmets and goggles, heard them gabbling away in a gutteral tone, saw them drinking from their bottles with their eyes to heaven. I gazed in amazement at these young men with corn-coloured hair. They poured some water on their handkerchiefs and cleaned up their faces a bit. Finally they leaned their machines against the wall, walked around and lined up to do a wee-wee. In their fists they held little pink sausages which looked soft and fragile, but the wee-wee was in fierce jets and I smelt it.

I must have moved on the wall, for one of the soldiers glanced up with fire in his eyes. What he saw of course was just one grey stockinged leg hanging down, topped by a garter and a thin white thigh. The man let out a huge laugh and grabbed my foot. I held onto the wall, shook my leg, yelled and finally he let me go. I was scarlet and terrified as I scampered off on the convent side of the wall. I hurled myself in the general direction of the kitchens shouting: 'They're here, the Germans are here!' I was soon held in the firm arms of Sister Wilhelmine, sobbing my heart out. 'Jesu, Mary, Joseph, pray for us,' she muttered.

That evening the convent was occupied. A handsome looking officer presented a wad of papers to the Mother Superior, clicking his heels and bowing, then waiting for her to finish reading. The troops took over three dormitories out of the five, half the classrooms, several rooms on the ground floor for the officers, and the grounds. Sister Wilhelmine acted as interpreter and it was agreed that the Germans could have the kitchens too provided they fed the sisters and the others. This meant the cooks among the sisters would have no contact with the men. Smiles all round. They were our he-men with human faces!

The evening service was longer than usual with the chaplain exhorting us to show courage, sacrifice and modesty. I saw Sister Wilhelmine crying; she came from Bavaria and was requisitioned as a secretary for the Kommandantur. She was a tall, pallid, plump woman who had not yet taken her vows.

Thereafter the establishment lost its habitual tranquillity to the sound of boots, raucous shouts, clipped orders, soldiers' songs and the gong. The smells changed, too, and we had boot polish, sauerkraut, beer and male sweat in our nostrils. The modest tones of our bell calling us to prayer had a hard time penetrating the confusion. We would go to chapel in long lines, our garments rustling, our fists holding our skirts in, our eyes demurely cast down under our black lace mantillas. Wherever we went there were men leaning against the walls, smoking and cackling, waving a casual hand at us. Their heavy facetious politeness hastened us on our way. For the rest of the summer holidays I stayed in a classroom on the third floor, sometimes looking out onto the grounds watching the young men in swimsuits lying in the sun playing football or doing physical jerks. They always seemed to be washing their things in big tubs, or looking after the racehorses they had stolen en route. The officers would take their ease among the apple trees. It was summer, it was the war and I was 13. I remember the breathless heat.

In the Autumn some of the girls came back as if nothing had happened but we averaged only 7 or 8 a class. During recreation we hung about in the small yard and the soldiers used to leer at us from their windows. When they began digging trenches in the lawns we knew they were there at least for the winter. I was glad to find two particular friends again, smart but shifty country girls, and in the dormitory at night we used to compare our breasts. At lights-out we closed the white curtains around our beds and slipped down in the freezing sheets to listen to the incomprehensible row kicked up by the men in their sleeping quarters: laughing, arguments, snoring. We got hold of a textbook on German and read it secretly, three of us in the one bed: '*Der Tee ist gut aber die Tasse ist zu klein ...*'

One night in the deep mid-winter, we were roused from slumber by a clanging alarm bell and cries of '*Schnell, Raus, schnell, schnell!*' In three minutes we had jumped out and run in our nightdresses, hair flying, to a trench-shelter the troops had allotted to us outside. We listened to the planes and the anti-aircraft fire and then returned meekly to our beds through twin lines of men, who were nudging each other and making remarks. We were like a line of geese. Officers would head our procession, and others would bring up the rear, smacking our bottoms whenever it suited them. The alerts seemed to get more frequent after a while, which was not surprising as we wore newly-acquired dressing gowns, blue for the girls and black for the sisters; they were quite fetching. We had rosaries in our pockets so that we didn't waste time looking for them.

We three friends used to inspect the trenches, and we found a first-aid kit buried in the ground. Behind it were a bottle of champagne and some cigarettes, which we sneaked up to the dormitory. Silently and conscientiously we got drunk under one of the beds. The next day we smoked the cigarettes in the toilet, playing the tart to each other. From the toilet we sent out our first messages starting impressively with '*Ich liebe dich*'. At night we would clench our bolsters between our legs and dream about the Germans.

Some of the sisters began using their shawls like model-girls at some fashion show, and tying sweet little bows under their chins with the mantillas. Wilhelmine quit her religious garb for mufti; these civilian clothes were formless and frumpy by today's standards but she had a way of tilting her hat over one eye that fooled no-one. When she was on duty in the dormitories she was specially tender when she scolded us for our dirty aprons and our badly gartered stockings; she used to stroke our necks in a furtive sort of way, teach us how to bite our lips to make them red and give us little flicks on the cheeks to make them glow. She had a funny manner, and seemed to envelop us, at the same time showing us how to keep ourselves upright and stick our budding breasts out. We let her caress us where she liked, and put curlers in our hair as the tiny ones looked on disapprovingly. I noticed that Wilhelmine had slimmed down quite a lot, her gaze appeared to shine and she often raised her eyes to heaven. Often she broke off dreamily in the middle of a sentence, and swooped up and down the dormitory with her skirt swaying this way and that.

One night when we were busy with another bottle of champagne we heard a noise and popped our heads out. Wilhelmine was completely naked in the moonlight, with her long hair over her body. She stroked her waist and her breasts, then sometimes put a hand between her legs, lifting it to her mouth and sucking it like a lollipop.

At the Liberation, we learned that Wilhelmine had had all her hair shaved off, and been paraded round the town before being brought back to the convent. Over-excited men threw her down in the main hall and kicked her. She spent three days and nights lying face down in the chapel, her arms spread out sideways. As we stared at her bare head we recited the rosary for her. The other sisters at length brought her something to drink, and she managed to get a few sips down before she slumped back to the floor.

Two years after the war she took her vows, wearing the customary white satin wedding dress. The Bride of Our Lord lay down as before with her arms out. Then her glorious golden locks, once more down to her shoulders, were again removed with a pair of scissors.

Lise Grandjouan

Shrimp Girl

All week I had been running around Maintenon getting things for the New Year party. On that afternoon of December 31, 1981, the hands on the clock were whirring round at twice their normal speed. I was like a wasp in a jam jar worrying how the devil I would get everything ready. But there was another reason why I was so het up. Ten very good friends were to be our guests and I wanted the dinner to be the best ever. Miraculously I was ready when they started to arrive and could even join in as my husband Laurent popped open the bottles of champagne we were serving as the aperitif. Thanks to Veuve Cliquot we embarked on the meal in joyous mood, making enough noise for a regiment.

The jokes, the jibes and the retorts made the evening a howling success, and I was delighted to find that Laurent was on the top of his form. After 21 years together it was absolutely marvellous that we could entertain so well, and still with the same freshness. As the meal drew to a close I jumped up and put a record on, wanting the mood to continue at the same pace. At the same time I kept thinking that another year was gone forever, one that might be better than the coming 12 months. I was fizzy and fuzzy.

Nonetheless I felt the perfect hostess and let everyone see how much I loved my man, while accepting a few dances from my friends' husbands. By 3 am we were all tipsy or worn out or both, when the front doorbell rang. This did not surprise me entirely, Laurent being a doctor. I went to open the door, preparing myself for the emergency call. In fact it was I who needed help, nearly fainting when I saw who was standing there in a dress suit. It was Michel, a young man who had walked out on me 25 years previously. Perhaps it was because he rocked on his heels and was shaking his head in that silly way, but I instantly recalled his penchant for Bordeaux wine. He stumbled over a few words and I drew him inside, telling Laurent to stick with the others and that I would look after Michel and explain later.

I took him into the dining room and alone we devoured each other with our eyes. He was still a head height above me, and as I gazed at him our past history flooded back into my mind. A big tear rolled down his left cheek and I bit my lip to keep myself from breaking down. I deliberately opened my eyes wide hoping that this would help too.

Within a minute I was to learn that he was not the worse for drink at all. He had called for a special reason, asking me to come with him to Paris for four to six months in connection with 'this bit of paper'. I had difficulty focussing but saw at once that it was a clinical analysis. We had last seen each other during my second year at pharmaceutical college. I was horrified by what I read; the scruffy piece of paper was a veritable death sentence, and the name and first name were definitely Michel's. There it was in black and white. He was to enter hospital tomorrow and I pulled myself together, noting the name of the establishment, the service, the phone number. I refrained from comment, gave him a warm smile and politely promised I would be there. He then left.

I was in a quandary. He had come to me for help and I knew what the analysis meant. But I was also a wife and mother and my family needed me. How could I possibly just clear off for months?

But I did clear off! I left everything and everyone! Nothing could hold me back when I'd thought it out, neither Laurent's supplications, nor the fear of wrecking our life, nor the tears of my appalled offspring, nor the innocent blue eyes of the baby who understood nothing.

I left in the train from Maintenon to Paris, with enough money in the bank to last six months. I was flying towards Michel, terrified at what the months ahead held for him, wanting me near him if the worst was to happen. But why me? Why did he want me to hold his hand and lead him to the Woman in Black, the ogress hungry for young male bodies?

I found a simple hotel close to the hospital, run by a

pleasant bald-headed man, and I called in on Michel every afternoon except Wednesdays. He didn't want me in the morning when there was too much going on; he got tired, of course, and no doubt tried to look as fresh as he could for our meetings. It was a fact that he always looked spruced up and handsome and smelling of Guerlain's Imperial when I arrived. I remembered him explaining to me how it was produced for Napoleon III. I recalled too how he liked me to wear lots of Vol de Nuit and kept me well supplied.

Michel was a very sick man, and the treatment was sapping his strength. My role was simplicity itself, to give him reassurance by being there when he woke. When that happened his lovely mint-coloured eyes bored into mine, and his long fine hands found their way to mine. He said little himself, occasionally asking me to run over the good times we had had. I skipped over the awkward incidents and stuck to the good times; I felt so terribly sorry for him.

Increasingly they gave him drugs to make him sleep. Often he dozed off while I was with him and, in the morbid atmosphere of the room, I had all the time in the world to relive the things that bound me to the hand I contemplated and squeezed.

I remembered a day long ago when I was a child. I was out shrimping, a jumper pulled anyhow over my bathing suit and a floppy old satchel slung round my waist, when I caught sight of a boy a few feet away lifting his fishing net out of the water. He had brown hair and eyes the colour of the green sea, knees like boxes and clothes and tackle straight off a postcard 50 years old. I had seen him at Sunday mass between a pair of plump women wearing fruit salad hats. I was keen to avoid all chat with him about the best spots for shrimps, and gradually eased away from him. About a minute later I heard him exclaim, and saw him squirming about with a leg apparently trapped. I ran over and shifted a large rock that had fallen down on his foot. We then went up the beach with him hopping along and leaning on my shoulder.

Eventually we got to Le Chateau, the large residence where he stayed. A governess with purple cheeks relieved me of my burden and thanked me. I got no cream cakes out of it and went off feeling annoyed at wasting good shrimping time. I was too innocent to realize that I had encountered my first love, that is, love had assumed the form of a body and a face. He hobbled along to our place the next day and thanked me rather formally; we were inseparable for the next 12 years.

Our games started with the beach, naturally, looking for different shellfish and shrimps. Then we went on bike rides and out in his boat. By some miracle he actually lived near me in the Paris suburbs, so that we just went on seeing each other. He always seemed to be dragging me along behind him because he was much taller and had longer legs, although was only a year older than I was.

It was not long before we found ourselves kissing, clumsily but passionately. I loved this forbidden fruit, and I know he did too, even if little was said between us. Our smooching sessions took place in secret hideouts, where we thought we were doing something really naughty. Michel was so handsome! It was curious how I never tried to show him off to my girl friends and make them writhe with jealousy. I remember I was constantly astonished when I got back home to find everything as before, with my parents going about their affairs exactly as before when I had come in from a Great Adventure involving no little risk.

As we grew up we never quite lost sight of each other; for example he used to meet me at the *lycee* and sometimes when I finished at the sports-ground. We spent hours putting the world to rights, the world of the adults of course. We were horrifed over the Soviet tanks as they rumbled into Budapest, even more horrified over the fighting in Algeria, especially when it dragged on and on.

Meanwhile we had to plan our careers. For Michel there was no choice, as his dad forced him into the HEC commercial college, after his brother who preceded him by a year got into the *Ecole de Chimie*. In their family it was industry from father to son, way back over the generations. As far as this generation of Duvergers was concerned, Michel and his brother were to take over a big glassworks, in charge of production and marketing respectively.

Michel took his studies seriously and never questioned the old man's decision, but he still found plenty of time to walk out with me and hold hands in the cinema.

A week or so before his 19th birthday, while I was asking him what he would like from me, he suddenly declared that the best present of all would be my consent to a three-day trip in a country house they had outside Fontaine-bleau. His jaw jutted out when he said it and his lower lip slid forward; I felt sure he would hit me if I said no. So I said yes. Afterwards I was worried so far we had not gone beyond light petting and I had always blocked his approaches, not least because I didn't want to get pregnant. Now he had me up against a wall, so to speak, with a trip that was to last from Thursday evening until Monday dawn. No doubt it was because I had just got through my exams and I felt heady with success that I agreed. The fact is that I worked out a story for my parents and confirmed my acceptance the next day.

We reached Le Bois-Charme under a leaden hot sky that June afternoon. The house was startling white and nestling in huge banks of flowers and circled with trees. Michel drove the 2 h.p. Citroen into a rickety old shed and then showed me round. The grounds contained lush, inviting lawns that anyone would want to lie on; these gave way to open fields of corn peppered with poppies *a la Monet*. 'The most beautiful bed in the world,' Michel pronounced, and pulled me down. Within seconds I was trapped under his muscled torso with the face of a wild beast looking down on mine, while the twigs and stones dug into my back through my skirt and blouse. He didn't kiss me, he bit me, and all over. I had asked for it by coming, and I bit back! Then we calmed down and stroked and fondled each other gently under the amber sky and cradled in the corn. I was helpless the moment he stopped hurrying me and I could gaze into his green eyes with the corn reflected in them, feel his honey skin, our mutual desire burning redder than the poppies.

'Not here,' he rasped suddenly, then got to his feet and hauled me up by my wrists. He charged across the lawn with me in tow protesting. I wanted to stop then and he kept saying 'Not here, not here.' Michel was a jungle cat pulling his mate where he wanted her, striding urgently with a supple tread to his lair. This frightened me and thrilled me at the same time, and I knew I wanted to make love as much as he did, knew I would let him, realized I was incapable of resistance now. I ran three paces to his one, not daring to make a fuss in case he changed his mind. Not to make it too easy I pretended reluctance as we scrunched up the gravel path and mounted the steps. We flashed through the kitchen and I asked for a glass of water and he said 'Not now!' Michel was the timid type, but he was making up for it now! He was going to have me, whatever I said, but when he started up the stairs and I saw the doors to a couple of bedrooms I could not help hesitating. My head was throbbing and I wanted to cry, though I could not have said why.

Behind the door on the right he removed my clothing and I simply gaped at him. Then he took his own off, and I was flung onto a satin eiderdown and kissed hungrily and more expertly as the moments passed. His thing was hard and I felt it nudging my thighs. I recall wondering where he learned all these techniques, then thought of a French teacher who told us that Adele and Victor Hugo did it nine times on their wedding night. Michel's strong legs prised mine apart and I saw his ponderous shaft only centimetres from my virgin flower. I believe I whimpered then, no doubt thinking it would hurt, and then he was forcing his penis through my fleece. I knew I was already moist and let myself go. Whereat desire was made flesh and our bodies were one. Michel took me with slow irregular thrusts and I simply let the sensations come, until an immense wave of joy unfurled itself, a sort of swelling that surged through me and drew the blood from my legs. I was weightless and groaning, rolling my head from side to side.

I, Francoise had lost my innocence for ever, but I was a true woman at last. The expression 'seventh heaven' floated into my mind and I told the god who now lay panting on top of me. He flopped off and lay by my side, and I was so overjoyed I knelt next to him and covered him with tiny kisses, sucking at his abdomen, burying my face into it while it rose and fell firmly under my nose and cheeks and eyes and mouth.

We descended the staircase in a glow, and my prince installed me in a deck chair. Michel took the lurching old car off to the village for food and drink. To this day I can see the smile he threw at me as he gave a little wave. I sank down into the deck chair, prostrate and with my eyes shut, pointing them towards the sun which was a soft pink through my eyelids. I was in wonderland, thinking about his 'I love you', just before he entered me, at the precise instant when it was needed.

So it was true, I thought, what people said about the 'teeth of fortune', meaning the tiny gap I had between the two middle teeth at the top. That was lucky, they said, and it was true! I could not sleep for happiness, and kept seeing those poppies that had really started it off. I kept seeing his pile-driver too!

For three days and four nights we thrashed about on that satin overlay, occasionally glimpsing the sun on the *terrasse* and grabbing steaks and stuff done on a wood fire. When we separated on the Monday morning I felt bursting with Michel, and when we met again three days later I still had him inside me!

We were lovers for three whole years, Michel coming to my 'couch' every night. We were sure it was for ever, for our bodies were made for each other and we had similar tastes in books, films, paintings and things we browsed over in antique shops. Both of us flew gaily through our exams, Michel completing the HEC and myself getting through the oral in second year pharmacy. We were a couple. We had crossed the Rubicon.

But it was not to last. The talkative, jokey, fascinating Michel turned sad. And I sensed that our heaven was turning sour. He started going to bed and to sleep quite early, he no longer suggested films or exhibitions. He used to make love to me without the essential endearments that go with the foreplay, but with an animal lust. I saw he was suffering but could not explain why. He seemed to be hunted, forlorn.

Then one morning his sister Catherine called, and for a

moment I thought something had happened to him. She told me their father was sending him to the United States on a special course for a year and it was all arranged. I frowned, unable to see why it was she who was telling me this. Then she released the bombshell: Michel's marriage was arranged too. Business is business! I believe Michel honestly fought to find a way out, but the paternal authority plus the poison his mother must have put in the soup, got the better of him.

I pleaded, choked, almost cried: 'I can't live without you, Michel, without your lips, without your hands.' To be truthful, I was less distraught over losing him as a life-long partner than over the end of our fun together. Only three hours earlier we had torn ourselves apart as we stumbled out of the crumpled bed where we had worn ourselves out in frenzied pleasure. No, it wasn't the wedding ring I missed, and yet I would have liked to do the wording on the invitation for him: 'Those Duverger bastards are happy to announce the marriage of their handsome Michel with the fat, turnip pie Mademoiselle Odile X, daughter of a pair of rats ...'

Odile was a piggy-bank with knobs on, above the belt! But below the belt no pleasure would issue forth, that's for sure. Michel's seed would lose itself in her vagina like a coin in a slot machine and out would come pimply puffy rag dolls.

That was our story, Michel's and mine. As he grew worse on his hospital bed, he slept longer and longer. Awake, he kept searching for my eyes, and then he was reassured. His luminous tender gaze was still there, and I felt that his translucid soul was trying to tell me something. I had to guess what it was. *Felix qui potuit rerum cogniscere causas*: happy the man who can penetrate the secret causes of things.

He uttered no word for weeks, and then the nice bald man at the hotel woke me saying the hospital had phoned. Michel was dead. I left at once, for Michel was no more and there was nothing more for me to do. That was up to the widow: 'Monsieur Louis Duverger and Madame deeply regret to inform you of the death of their son Michel after a long illness during which he refused to have anything to do with his family. The deplorable widow wishes to contact a successor with surplus money and long arms to go round her fat waist ...' The sow!

To lose one man, to paraphrase Oscar Wilde, may be regarded as a misfortune; to lose both would look like carelessness. It struck me that I had plenty to lose after a five-month absence. I paid the hotel bill in a state of mounting panic and ordered a taxi for the Gare Montparnasse. There was no train for two hours, worse luck, and I hung about at the station, bought an apple pie and a cup of coffee, then another coffee. My hands were shaking and I nearly phoned Laurent but thought better of it. With still more than an hour to go, I was as miserable as a day without love. What if another woman had taken over in my absence, using my saucepans, making my beds, sleeping in my bed with my man? Oh no, Laurent wouldn't do that. After all, I had been as pure as driven snow for five months, something I would not have imagined possible before. No, that would not be negligence, that would be the death of me!

As the train rushed past Versailles Castle I thought of my own little Versailles, of our castle together, Laurent and me. Oh God, I always believed in you, please let Laurent be waiting, please don't let me lose him too.

Rambouillet – Maintenon – the first taxi – 'Rue des Acacias please.' Then I was at the intercom, speaking in a cracked voice. Laurent answered and pushed the button, the gate clicked and I walked up the drive between the chestnut trees. And there he was! Sitting on a garden chair, frowning, scowling even. Perhaps there really was someone else.

I let my case down and my eyes misted over, but not enough to prevent me seeing him getting up and almost run to me. Oh thank God! He held me tight and we both cried as I clung to his arms. I opened the front door and we went in, straight up the stairs. I knew every square inch of those stairs, had gone up them so often without realizing they were the pathway to the stars. I opened the bedroom door and Laurent closed it and locked it, Oh yes, darling, let's make love, I want to so badly. Now, please, please! Take me on your Jumbo Jet!

Mister Wilde can get lost, as my kids would say.

As for the shrimp girl, the girl among the poppies, the smart woman in her 40's who went away into the dark winter's night, she has not come this far without knowing she can stifle *that* love.

I have been working at it for too long and my deathbed thoughts will not be of you, Michel.

But, good God, don't call us too early, Laurent and I. Give us time to savour some more of those long nights alone, just the two of us, heart to heart.

Francoise Baranger